"Absolutely *nothing* is more important in a church than the DNA of the leadership culture. The healthiest churches I know are those that are led by pastors and elders who are captured by the gospel, smitten with Jesus, and transformed by God's grace. Bob Thune's new book, *Gospel Eldership*, presents a vision and roadmap for cultivating this kind of leadership culture."

> **Scotty Ward Smith,** Teacher in Residence, West End Community Church, Nashville, TN

"I've lost count of the number of times that pastors, church planters, and seminary students have asked me for a practical, hands-on, gospel-centered, and challenging resource for elders-in-training and current elders in churches. The book you have in your hands is that resource—finally! *Gospel Eldership* provides much-needed and long-awaited formation for servant leadership in our churches!"

> **Gregg R. Allison,** Professor, The Southern Baptist Theological Seminary; pastor, Sojourn Community Church, Louisville, KY; Secretary, Evangelical Theological Society; author of *Historical Theology, Sojourners and Strangers*, and *Roman Catholic Theology and Practice*

"There is so much confusion about how the church should be governed and led. I love how clear and compelling Bob has made the high calling of being a pastor in *Gospel Eldership*. I can't wait to use this incredible resource in our church and I would encourage you to do the same."

> **Darrin Patrick,** Lead Pastor, The Journey, St. Louis; Vice President, Acts 29; chaplain to St. Louis Cardinals; author of *Church Planter, The Dude's Guide to Manhood*; coauthor of *The Dude's Guide to Marriage*

"Bob Thune brings us gospel formation over information with a bias for soul depth, not breadth. Buy *Gospel Eldership* for your next elder candidate process—or better yet, buy it for current elders to start a journey toward greater honesty, openness, and holiness. Your church will thank you for it."

> **Daniel Montgomery,** Lead Pastor, Sojourn Community Church, Louisville, KY; founder of the Sojourn Network; author of *Faithmapping, PROOF*, and *Leadership Mosaic*

"It is noble to aspire to eldership. However, transforming elder aspiration into godly, prepared pastoral service demands more than desire. It requires hard work—the work of personal discipline and a power outside of self. Godly elders depend on gospel power, the sufficiency and excellency of Jesus Christ applied to every aspect of life and ministry. *Gospel Eldership* will help you cultivate elder character, skill, and doctrine that depends on Jesus. I have used *Gospel Eldership* in several rounds of elder training and appreciate it more with each use. Our elder candidates often comment on its usefulness and convicting power. I will continue to use *Gospel Eldership* with enthusiasm as we train godly, gospel-motivated men for pastoral service."

Jonathan Dodson, Lead Pastor, City Life Church; author of *Gospel-Centered Discipleship* and *The Unbelievable Gospel*

GOSPEL ELDERSHIP

EQUIPPING A NEW GENERATION OF SERVANT LEADERS

Robert H. Thune

New
Growth
Press
WWW.NEWGROWTHPRESS.COM

New Growth Press, Greensboro, NC 27404
Copyright © 2016 by Robert H. Thune

Cover Design: Faceout Books, faceoutstudio.com
Interior Design and Typesetting: Lisa Parnell, lparnell.com

ISBN 978-1-942572-61-9 (Print)
ISBN 978-1-942572-62-6 (eBook)

Printed in India

27 26 25 24 23 22 21 20   8 9 10 11 12

CONTENTS

ACKNOWLEDGMENTS

I am deeply grateful to the following people, for helping to shape both this material and my own heart:

To my wife Leigh: I'm humbled by your love and blessed by your friendship. Thanks for leaning into all the joys and trials of church leadership with courage and grace.

To my fellow pastors in the Acts 29 Network: Thanks for the rich gospel brotherhood you've provided over the past decade of planting churches together.

To the elders of Coram Deo Church, both past and present: I love you men. Thanks for the joy of leading Jesus's church alongside you.

To Darrin Patrick, John Ryan, David Fairchild, Scott Thomas, and Matt Chandler: Thanks for making time over the past decade to serve a young leader trying to find his way. You have encouraged me and served me in ways I don't deserve.

To Kevin Cawley, Josh Kouri, and Will Walker: Thanks for fighting for an uncommon sort of brotherhood and friendship. I hope the principles in this resource will help others taste just a little bit of the synergy and joy we've known together.

To Alex Strauch: Thanks for helping us go "back to the Bible" in our thinking about church leadership. We're all standing on your shoulders.

To my dad: Thanks for being a faithful, reliable, Christlike spiritual leader in both the home and the church. So much of what I know about leadership I learned from you.

INTRODUCTION:
WHAT IS AN ELDER?

Whether formal or informal, recognized or unrecognized, leadership is a given in any church. In fact, leadership is a given in any human society. When kids play football on the playground, someone picks the teams. When volunteers get together to clean up a neighborhood park, someone organizes the initiative. When friends get together for a book club, someone chooses the book and plans the discussion. Every human community has some form of leadership.

Right now you're looking at a resource on church leadership. Based on that fact alone, I can deduce that you have some interest in church leadership, or at least, one of the elders in your church sees leadership potential in you. What I don't know are your current convictions about church leadership, your past experiences with church leadership, or your present context. So let's start with a basic observation we can all agree on:

Every church has leaders.

Starting from that universal reality, the real question we need to ask is *What **kind** of leaders should the church have?* Did God intend his church to be led by just anyone? Or did he give some outline, some matrix, some set of instructions for church leadership?

As we answer this question, we repeatedly see in the Bible an emphasis on a group of leaders referred to as elders, bishops, or overseers. For instance,

> When they had preached the gospel to that city and had made many disciples, they returned to Lystra and to Iconium and to Antioch, strengthening the souls of the disciples, encouraging them to continue in the faith, and saying that through many tribulations we must enter the kingdom of God. And when they had appointed *elders* for them in every church, with prayer and fasting they committed them to the Lord in whom they had believed. (Acts 14:21–23)

> Let the *elders* who rule well be considered worthy of double honor, especially those who labor in preaching and teaching. (1 Timothy 5:17)

> This is why I left you in Crete, so that you might put what remained into order, and appoint *elders* in every town as I directed you. (Titus 1:5)

> Is anyone among you sick? Let him call for the *elders* of the church, and let them pray over him, anointing him with oil in the name of the Lord. (James 5:14)

> The saying is trustworthy: If anyone aspires to the office of *overseer*, he desires a noble task. Therefore an *overseer* must be above reproach. . . . (1 Timothy 3:1–2)

God intends for his church to be led by godly leaders known as *elders*. So what *is* an elder?

An elder is a pastor. Many of us only apply the title of "pastor" to those in full-time vocational ministry. But in the Bible, the terms *elder* (*presbuteros*), *pastor* (*poimen*), and *bishop* (*episkopos*) are used interchangeably to refer to the same person or group of people. Two particular New Testament texts make this abundantly clear.

> From Miletus he sent to Ephesus and called to him the *elders* [*presbuterous*] of the church. And when they had come to him, he said to them . . . "Be on guard for yourselves and for all the flock, among which the Holy Spirit has made you *overseers* [*episkopous*], to *shepherd* [*poimainein*] the church of God which He purchased with His own blood." (Acts 20:17–18, 28 NASB)

> Therefore, I exhort the *elders* [*presbuterous*] among you, as your fellow elder and witness of the sufferings of Christ, and a partaker also of the glory that is to be revealed, *shepherd* [*poimanate*] the flock of God among you, exercising *oversight* [*episkopountes*] not under compulsion, but voluntarily, according to the will of God (1 Peter 5:1–2 NASB).

In my household, I have the titles of husband (to my wife), father (to my children), and head of household (to the IRS). But those titles are all various aspects of one role or office: the leader of a family. The same is true in the Bible. One office—the office of local church elder—is referred to under three titles: elder, pastor, and overseer/bishop. Some elders may serve the church full time (those we usually call "pastors"), while other elders may serve as lay volunteers. But biblically speaking, elders are pastors and pastors are elders.

An elder is a pacesetter. The elders of the New Testament churches were not mere figureheads; they were leaders, pacesetters, and disciple-makers. Scripture sees elders as competent, committed, mature leaders who teach (1 Timothy 3:2), rebuke (Titus 1:9), rule (1 Timothy 5:17), guard sound doctrine (Titus 1:9), do evangelism (Titus 1:8), deal with difficult people (Titus 1:10–14), and raise up other leaders (2 Timothy 2:2).

An elder is *not* merely a faithful, reliable Christian who shows up to meetings and votes. Rather, an elder sets the pace for the rest of the church. Elders are leaders of strength, wisdom, and integrity, whose lives and character are worthy of being imitated and reproduced in every Christian.

An elder is a man. We live in a very egalitarian culture today, where any distinction in gender roles arouses suspicion. But the Bible unapologetically makes such distinctions. Is this because the Bible is a repressive, patriarchal text that needs to be updated and adapted to fit modern sensibilities? Or is it because God actually made men and women differently, to fulfill distinct but complementary roles?

The Bible's vision of the relationship between the sexes is one of rich interdependence (1 Corinthians 11:11–12). God designed men and women to complement one another as his image-bearers (Genesis 1:26–31; 2:15–25), and his design includes differing roles for men and women in the home and in the church (1 Timothy 2:11–3:5). Men are given the responsibility of headship in the home and in the church, which means that the office of elder-pastor is to be filled by men. This is not a matter of empowering men and restricting women, but rather of freeing both sexes to enjoy the beautiful, God-glorifying harmony of a robust interdependence. *Complementarianism* is the theological term for this viewpoint. Men and women are complementary in their God-given design and roles, with men bearing the responsibility for spiritual leadership in the home and church.

This book is unapologetically complementarian in its approach. If you are still forming your convictions on this matter, I invite you to read this study with an open mind. And I urge you to ponder this question: If the men in your church looked like the men this resource envisions, would you have any reason not to trust, respect, and affirm their leadership? To further your theological formation on this important issue, consult the resources listed in the endnotes.[1]

Elders, then, are the male leaders of the church who serve as pastors and pacesetters. But we must say more. If a church is to be healthy, its elders must be men who are *grounded and rooted in the gospel*. That is the crucial gap in many churches today, and that is the weakness that this book is designed to address.

Many resources on church leadership seem consumed with church management, church structures, and church governance—as though the most important thing elders do is hold meetings and vote. Almost nothing has been written about the quality of spiritual life an elder must have *as an elder*. Of course, there are many good books about spiritual formation, and many helpful resources designed to facilitate basic Christian discipleship. But few of these resources are targeted *specifically at church leaders*. Is it not true that leaders experience unique temptations, challenges, and struggles? And is it not true that for a church to go deep in the gospel, its leaders must be deep in the gospel? That's the vision and the goal behind *Gospel Eldership*.

In my experience, it's possible to be very old in the faith and yet tragically young in the gospel. If the gospel truly is "the power of God for salvation" (Romans 1:16) and is constantly "bearing fruit and growing" within us (Colossians 1:6 NIV), then elders must be strong in the gospel. They must know their own heart idolatry and how the good news of the gospel applies to it. And they must have a sense of "gospel fluency" so that they can swiftly, effectively, and clearly apply the gospel to others. Those are the kind of leaders that I'm seeking to develop with this book.

So if you're curious about that kind of leadership; if you're seeking to *be* a leader like that; or if you're seeking to raise up and release those kinds of leaders, this book is for you.

HOW TO USE THIS RESOURCE

This book can be used in a number of different ways. It's designed to be adaptable for different settings and contexts. But it's written with three primary audiences in mind.

1. Current elders who want to deepen their theological understanding and their gospel fluency.
2. Elders-in-training who are progressing through a season of learning and examination.

3. Christians who are seeking to better understand the Bible's teaching about local church leadership.

From my experience, *you'll* see the best results when this book is used as a small-group study. Ideally, a current elder or spiritual mentor should lead a group of emerging leaders through the content. This way, the written material serves as a springboard for the more important work of personal mentorship and spiritual formation. The following is a suggested weekly plan for using the resource in this way:

1. Have each participant read the article and work through the exercise independently during the week.
2. Come together as a group for 90–120 minutes to
    a. Talk through the discussion questions.
    b. Share what you learned in the exercises.
    c. Cultivate honest, transformative relationships with one another.

The focus of this group time is not information, but formation. Therefore, each participant should come ready to share openly and honestly. You don't necessarily need to talk through every single question (though sometimes that's fruitful). Rather, feel free to hone in on whatever aspects of the lesson are most thought provoking and character shaping to your particular group.

As you study, keep in mind that this is a spiritual formation resource. It's not a theology textbook, an academic dissertation, or a full-scale biblical exposition. At the back of this guide, I've included a short bibliography for those interested in going deeper into some of the theological literature surrounding eldership and church leadership.

WHAT TO EXPECT

Expect to be challenged. This resource is not intended to reinforce what you already know, but to reshape and reform your understanding of church leadership. Along the way, you'll be challenged and provoked.

Expect to be surprised. This book is intended to provoke self-discovery and to uncover heart idolatry, sin, and selfishness you may not be aware of. This is a *good* thing because it invites you into deeper partnership and fellowship with the Holy Spirit! But it's also a *surprising* thing because self-awareness has a way of sneaking up on you when you least expect it.

Expect a deeper level of community. If you work through this resource with a small group of leaders, as recommended above, the Holy Spirit will forge tight bonds of friendship and brotherhood. Be ready to know and be known in ways that go far beyond your current experience.

Expect a deeper love for Christ and his church. As I've written this resource, this is what I've prayed for. I hope this resource builds your theological knowledge and helps you grasp some practical components of eldership. But more importantly, I hope it awakens a sense of worship and conviction within you as you seek to become the leader God intends *you* to be.

lesson

1

SERVANT LEADERSHIP

OBJECTIVE

To examine how Jesus's model of leadership differs from the world's default mode of leadership, and how Jesus makes this sort of leadership possible.

SCRIPTURE READING

- Mark 10:32–45

ARTICLE

When you think of Jesus, do you think of him as the most effective leader who's ever lived?

Eldership is leadership. Good elders must be good leaders. And when it comes to leadership, we tend to look to the bookstore, the boardroom, or the blogosphere. We seek out mentors who have succeeded in the business world or led large ministries. We envision Jesus as a Savior, a sage, a Galilean miracle-worker—but not as the Leader of leaders.

But if Jesus really does "uphold the universe by the word of his power" (Hebrews 1:3); if "by him all things were created" (Colossians 1:16); if in him "are hidden all the treasures of wisdom and knowledge" (Colossians 2:3), then clearly he knows everything about everything. He's the most brilliant leadership expert ever. He knows more than the most successful CEO, the sharpest leadership consultant, the most compelling movement leader. What Jesus has to teach us about leadership is life-altering. And "leadership experts" have been rediscovering it for centuries.

THE DEFAULT PARADIGM

Jesus's instructions about leadership stand in stark contrast to the status quo. The world's default model of leadership, practiced over centuries and across cultures, is about *being served*. There's a hierarchy, and the leader is at the top. The followers serve the will of the leader, fulfill the desires of the leader, and further the interests of the leader. When God's people asked for a king, he warned them about the reality of this kind of leadership.

> "These will be the ways of the king who will reign over you: he will take your sons and appoint them to his chariots and to be his horsemen and to run before his chariots. . . . He will take your daughters to be perfumers and cooks and bakers. He will take the best of your fields and vineyards and olive orchards and give them to his servants. He will take the tenth of your grain and of your vineyards and give it to his officers and to his servants. He will take your male servants and female servants and the best of your young men and your donkeys, and put them to his work. He will take the tenth of your flocks, and you shall be his slaves." (1 Samuel 8:11–17)

This top-down vision of leadership is so ingrained in us that it's enshrined in popular proverbs: "To the victor go the spoils"; "It's lonely at the top"; "The cream always rises."

Jesus's disciples were well schooled in this paradigm of leadership. They envisioned Jesus's kingdom as more of the same. And they wanted to make sure they had a place at the top.

> And James and John, the sons of Zebedee, came up to him and said to him, "Teacher, we want you to do for us whatever

we ask of you." And he said to them, "What do you want me to do for you?" And they said to him, "Grant us to sit, one at your right hand and one at your left, in your glory." Jesus said to them, "You do not know what you are asking. Are you able to drink the cup that I drink, or to be baptized with the baptism with which I am baptized?" And they said to him, "We are able." And Jesus said to them, "The cup that I drink you will drink, and with the baptism with which I am baptized, you will be baptized, but to sit at my right hand or at my left is not mine to grant, but it is for those for whom it has been prepared." And when the ten heard it, they began to be indignant at James and John. (Mark 10:35–41)

In response to this request, Jesus turned the conventional thinking about leadership on its head. He introduced a whole new paradigm of leadership.

And Jesus called them to him and said to them, "You know that those who are considered rulers of the Gentiles lord it over them, and their great ones exercise authority over them. But it shall not be so among you. But whoever would be great among you must be your servant, and whoever would be first among you must be slave of all. For even the Son of Man came not to be served but to serve, and to give his life as a ransom for many." (Mark 10:42–45)

Jesus is *prescribing* for his disciples the kind of leadership they ought to practice, and he's also *describing* what he himself has come to do. Jesus expects his followers to be *servant leaders*. And he's come to make them just that. As the Chief Servant, he will give his life as a ransom to deliver us from selfish leadership and to free us to also perform servant leadership.

So, how does a "Jesus way of leadership" become a reality in us?

JESUS IS OUR EXAMPLE

First, Jesus is our example. He is the ultimate Servant Leader. He is the one we are to emulate. He is our model, our archetype, our pattern. "If I then, your Lord and Teacher, have washed your feet, you also ought to wash one another's feet. For I have given you an example, that you also should do just as I have done to you" (John 13:14–15).

Following Jesus's example means we jettison our false, flawed, self-advancing concepts of leadership. We embrace servant leadership as good, true, and beautiful. And then we *decide* to pursue it. We commit to it. We apprentice ourselves to Jesus and resolve that we will become servant leaders.

JESUS IS OUR SUBSTITUTE

Once we decide to follow Jesus's path of servant leadership, we begin to come face-to-face with the selfishness and sinfulness deep within us. Jesus's way of leading is impossible! It is contrary to the bent of our hearts. We want power. We want control. We want comfort, ease, and convenience. We want to be liked, needed, appreciated. We want to do what works for us. We want to be served rather than to serve.

This is why the gospel is foundational to Christian leadership! To flawed and fallen leaders, the gospel proclaims: "Rejoice! Jesus has come to redeem you." Jesus is not just our *model*; he is our *mediator*. The Son of Man came to serve selfish, greedy, flawed leaders. He died for us so that we might live for him. Our hope is not in our excellent servant leadership; our hope is in Jesus's perfect servanthood toward those who acknowledge their lack and their need.

JESUS IS OUR POWER

When weak leaders depend on a strong Christ, he does not just forgive their sins; he empowers them with his renewing grace. The Bible uses the metaphor of "pouring" to describe how generously God gives his Holy Spirit to his people through Jesus: "He saved us . . . by the washing of regeneration and renewal of the Holy Spirit, *whom he poured out on us richly* through Jesus Christ our Savior" (Titus 3:5–6). Whatever you lack, the Spirit has. Whatever you need, the Spirit can provide.

Paradoxically, then, the most servant-hearted leaders are those who are most aware of their struggles with servanthood. Why? Because these leaders are constantly going to Christ for fresh strength. They are constantly depending on the Spirit. They are constantly in lack, constantly in need, and therefore constantly experiencing God's renewing grace. The late seminary professor and pastor C. John Miller summarized the good news of the gospel using two phrases[1]:

- ***Cheer up! You're worse than you think!*** Your failures and flaws are even deeper than you know. Your capacity for servant leadership is smaller than you imagine. Your selfishness is stronger than you've realized. But....
- ***Cheer up! The gospel is far greater than you can imagine!*** God is not constrained by your limitations! God uses the weak, the flawed, the powerless. God loves to pour out his Spirit on humble leaders who acknowledge their need.

CONCLUSION

Gospel leadership is servant leadership; and servant leadership drives us back to the gospel. We cannot be the servant leaders Jesus commands us to be without believing the good news of the gospel. Likewise, we cannot believe the gospel without being moved toward greater servanthood. This cycle of renewal brings life and joy and fruitfulness to our leadership.

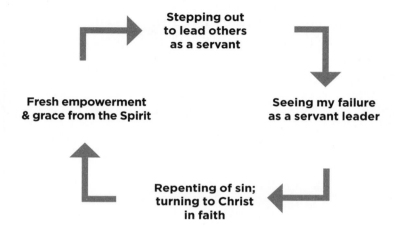

DISCUSSION QUESTIONS

1. What aspects of the world's model of leadership do you find attractive and compelling? What is it about those models that appeal to you?

2. Reread Mark 10:32–45. In what ways do you see the "glory hunger" of James and John playing out in your own calling or aspiration toward eldership?

3. "Following Jesus's example means . . . we embrace servant leadership . . . and then we *decide* to pursue it. We commit to it." Have you resolved to be a servant leader? In what ways? If you haven't, what are your hesitations? How will you establish this commitment in a traceable and verifiable way, so it can be affirmed by others and revisited by you?

4. The article mentions power, control, comfort, convenience, and approval as some of the self-interested motives involved in leadership. There are others. What self-interested motives do you see in your own leadership? How do they manifest themselves in your leadership? Cite specific examples.

5. Why is God's grace toward you in Christ good news *right now*? What aspects of his grace, mercy, and provision are you most thankful for after reading this article?

6. Where do you want to see a fuller manifestation of the Holy Spirit's power in your leadership? Describe it.

7. What further questions does this lesson raise for you?

EXERCISE

"KNOW THYSELF"

I say to everyone among you not to think of himself more highly than he ought to think, but to think with sober judgment. (Romans 12:3)

Leadership can be selfish without appearing to be so. The most obvious types of selfishness are . . . well, obvious. But there are deeper and more subtle expressions of self-interest that hinder us from real servant leadership. One of these subtle expressions of selfishness is the tendency for leaders to work out their own insecurities in the midst of leadership. For example,

- A leader who fears disapproval may use leadership in order to be liked.
- A leader who fears uncertainty may use leadership in order to gain a sense of control.
- A leader who fears vulnerability may use leadership as a way to "perform" in front of others and avoid being known deeply.
- A leader who fears failure may use leadership as a way to avoid risk.

This exercise is designed to help you begin to uncover and reflect upon some of your own insecurities, and see how they manifest themselves in your current leadership style.

PERSONAL REFLECTION

Take some time to think about and write down short answers to these questions:

- What are you most afraid of as a leader?

- In your leadership, what do you seek to avoid at all costs?

- What *must* you have as a leader in order to be satisfied?

- What makes you angry or sad? Why?

- What voices do you hear in your head? (Write them down; record the contours of your self-talk.)

- "If people knew _____ , they wouldn't follow me." What goes in the blank? Why do you think it's true?

Now, reflect on what you've written. Can you see how you use leadership to assuage your own doubts, fears, and insecurities?

- Are you *posturing*—pretending to be someone you're not?
- Are you *performing*—working hard to make yourself acceptable to God and others?
- Are you *panicking*—leading out of frenzy and anxiety rather than out of humble, restful confidence in God?
- Are you *passive*—avoiding certain aspects of leadership out of pride (I shouldn't have to do that) or fear (I don't know if I can do that)?

GOSPEL APPLICATION

In Jesus Christ, God accepts you and welcomes you just as you are. He knows everything about you. He is aware of all your under-confidence and overconfidence, all your pride and fear, all your sin and selfishness—and he delights in you anyway, because of Jesus! There's nothing you can do as a leader to make him love you more, and nothing you can do as a leader to make him love you less. He invites you to come to him, right now, acknowledging everything you've written and turning to him for fresh provision, power, and hope.

The core sin under every other sin is *unbelief*—the refusal to rest in the promises, assurances, and truths of the gospel. In closing, reflect on the following questions, and turn to Jesus with each of your answers:

- How do your responses above show unbelief? What specific biblical truths are you treating as untrue?

- How do your responses above show self-protection? How are you avoiding really *needing* Jesus as Savior?

- How do your responses above show self-reliance? How are you avoiding complete dependence on the Holy Spirit?

- Are you willing to acknowledge your selfishness and go to Christ, needy and weak, for power and provision? Do so now. (Then, when you meet to discuss this exercise with others, do so together.)

lesson

2

A BIBLICAL APPROACH TO CHURCH LEADERSHIP

OBJECTIVE

To consider three common models of church leadership and contrast them with a biblical understanding of leadership.

SCRIPTURE READING

- Acts 20:1–38

ARTICLE

All theology is contextual. Any time we "do theology," we seek to apply the Bible's teaching to a specific area of concern, to answer a question that's been raised by our environment or experience.

Therefore, as we set out to study the topic of eldership, we must acknowledge that we do so in a context—twenty-first-century American evangelical Christianity—that is rife with competing models of church leadership. It's crucial for us to rightly understand the Bible's teaching on the subject. In this lesson, we'll contrast the biblical model of church leadership with three other models that are unfortunately quite common in our culture.

THE BIBLICAL MODEL

According to the Bible, *the church is to be led by a plurality of called, qualified men known as elders.* Let's examine each aspect of this definition.

A PLURALITY OF MEN

The Bible consistently speaks of elders in terms of *plurality*. For instance: "When [Paul and Barnabas] had appointed *elders* for them in every church, with prayer and fasting, they committed them to the Lord in whom they had believed" (Acts 14:23). Likewise, in Titus 1:5 (NASB): "For this reason I left you in Crete, that you would set in order what remains and appoint *elders* in every city as I directed you." Even Paul, who was an apostle with a capital A, submitted his own ministry and calling to the elders in Jerusalem. "Then after fourteen years I went up again to Jerusalem with Barnabas, taking Titus along with me. I went up because of a revelation and set before *them* (though privately before those who seemed influential) the gospel that I proclaim among the Gentiles, in order to make sure I was not running or had not run in vain" (Galatians 2:1–2).

A properly functioning biblical church is led by *a plurality of leaders.* Some of them may serve in a full-time, vocational capacity, receiving their financial income from the church (1 Timothy 5:17–18; 1 Corinthians 9:7–14). Others may serve in a volunteer capacity, receiving their income from another job. One of them may have a "first among equals" role, while others may serve in less visible ways according to their gifting and calling. But whatever the nuances of its specific application, the biblical model of church leadership demands that qualified pastor-elders serve *together* as the spiritual leaders of the church, shepherding the flock and sharing responsibility, authority, and accountability as a team.

In a church-planting or pioneering missions context, one man often serves as the lone elder until other qualified men are raised up. This is commensurate with Paul's own ministry; he and his missionary team had to *make disciples in Crete in the first place* before he could leave Titus behind to "set in order what remains and appoint elders" (Titus 1:5). But even in this early "apostolic band" stage of church planting, a good leader should pray, work, and labor to raise up additional elders from within the church as quickly as possible.

CALLED MEN

"Called" is a loaded word, isn't it? It's been used to justify all sorts of nonsense: "The Lord is calling me to _____." And yet, no matter how abused and mistreated this idea is, it captures something very fundamental about how the Spirit of God works. Paul says to Timothy, "If anyone *aspires* to the office of overseer, he desires a noble task" (1 Timothy 3:1). Elders *aspire* to the office. They feel a sort of internal compulsion. They are provoked by the Holy Spirit to pursue the office.

But there is more to calling than a mere subjective interest. Dave Harvey tells of a church member who "sat across from his pastor testifying that he'd received a 'call to ministry.' . . . Then he informed the pastor he would be leaving the church in search of his ministry. So is that what happens? God speaks so loudly to a man that other voices become unnecessary?"[1] On the contrary, Harvey observes, "if you're called to pastoral ministry, you're called to the church. . . . [I]dentifying called men, evaluating their call, assessing their character, and positioning them to be fruitful in their call . . . [is] the responsibility of the local church."[2] This is symbolized in the biblical practice of "laying hands" on a new elder, representing his commissioning by God and the church (1 Timothy 5:22).

For this reason, some churches and church-planting agencies use the word *commended* rather than *called*. *Commended* implies that others have evaluated and affirmed a man's calling. A calling to eldership is not merely a subjective aspiration; it's an aspiration that has been tested and confirmed by other godly leaders in the context of a local church community.

QUALIFIED MEN

It's not enough for elders to be called; they must also be *qualified.* Since the people of the church are instructed to submit to the elders (Hebrews 13:17), God demands that elders be the type of people who are worthy of trust and submission. He protects the flock by laying out clear scriptural guidelines for all who wish to serve as elders.

> The saying is trustworthy: If anyone aspires to the office of overseer, he desires a noble task. Therefore an overseer must be above reproach, the husband of one wife, sober-minded, self-controlled, respectable, hospitable, able to teach, not a drunkard, not violent but gentle, not quarrelsome, not a lover of money. He must manage his own household well, with all dignity keeping his children submissive, for if someone does not know how to manage his own household, how will he care for God's church? He must not be a recent convert, or he may become puffed up with conceit and fall into the condemnation of the devil. Moreover, he must be well thought of by outsiders, so that he may not fall into disgrace, into a snare of the devil. (1 Timothy 3:1–7)

> Appoint elders in every town as I directed you—if anyone is above reproach, the husband of one wife, and his children are believers and not open to the charge of debauchery or insubordination. For an overseer, as God's steward, must be above reproach. He must not be arrogant or quick-tempered or a drunkard or violent or greedy for gain, but hospitable, a lover of good, self-controlled, upright, holy, and disciplined. He must hold firm to the trustworthy word as taught, so that he may be able to give instruction in sound doctrine and also to rebuke those who contradict it. (Titus 1:5b–9)

These texts lay out *qualifications*, not preferences. These are not traits that are nice for an elder to have; these are traits an elder *must* have. These are the benchmarks against which every potential elder must be measured. If a man does not meet these qualifications, he is not fit to serve in the office of elder.

KNOWN AS ELDERS

In the Bible, the terms *elder (presbuteros), pastor (poimen),* and *bishop (episkopos)* are *all used interchangeably to refer to the same person or group of people.* There are not elders, and then pastors, and then bishops. Rather, an elder = a pastor = a bishop. As noted in the Introduction, two particular New Testament texts make this abundantly clear.

> From Miletus he sent to Ephesus and called to him the elders [*presbuterous*] of the church. And when they had come to him, he said to them. . . . "Be on guard for yourselves and for all the flock, among which the Holy Spirit has made you overseers [*episkopous*], to shepherd [*poimainein*] the church of God which He purchased with His own blood." (Acts 20:17–18, 28 NASB)

> Therefore, I exhort the elders [*presbuterous*] among you, as your fellow elder and witness of the sufferings of Christ, and a partaker also of the glory that is to be revealed, shepherd [*poimanate*] the flock of God among you, exercising oversight [*episkopountes*] not under compulsion, but voluntarily, according to the will of God. (1 Peter 5:1–2 NASB)

Just as in my household I have the titles of husband (to my wife), father (to my children), and head of household (to the IRS). Those titles are all various aspects of the role of leader of a family. Similarly, in the church, the office of elder is referred to under various titles. The term *elder* describes the man "with reference to his dignity and standing (older); *bishop* describing the man with reference to his function and duty (oversight). . . . [T]he chief role of the pastor is feeding the flock through teaching, a role clearly assigned to bishops/overseers in 1 Timothy 3:2 ("An elder must be . . . apt to teach") and to elders in Titus 1:9 ("He will be able both to exhort in sound doctrine and to refute those who contradict"). This suggests that *pastor* is another name for *elder* and overseer."[3]

In conclusion, the Bible teaches that *the church is to be led by a plurality of called, qualified men known as elders.*

FLAWED MODELS OF CHURCH LEADERSHIP

Now that we've considered the biblical model of church leadership, let's contrast it with three models of church leadership that are widely practiced, but are biblically unjustifiable. To identify these models as flawed is not to say that the Holy Spirit doesn't work through them! Thankfully, he does. But if we're going to return to a biblical model of church governance, we need to speak honestly about where other models fall short.

MODEL #1: THE "ANOINTED LEADER" MODEL

The first faulty model of leadership is the model of the "anointed leader." In churches with this form of leadership, the pastor is "God's man" who has the Holy Spirit's blessing and is seen to be a virtually untouchable and unquestionable spiritual leader. He usually practices a solo model of leadership, shunning peer accountability and often ruling with an authoritarian spirit.

Biblically, there are a number of problems with this model.

1. **Elders are always spoken of in plurality**. As noted above, the Bible always mentions *elders* in plurality. For instance, Acts 14:23: "When [Paul and Barnabas] had appointed *elders* for them in every church, with prayer and fasting they committed them to the Lord in whom they had believed."

2. **The Bible warns of false teachers who will seek power**. "I know that after my departure fierce wolves will come in among you, not sparing the flock; and from among your own selves will arise men speaking twisted things, to draw away the disciples after them" (Acts 20:29–30). Not every "anointed leader" is a wolf. But without true peer accountability, there is a strong temptation to seek power in this model.

3. **Apostleship is a spiritual gift, not a title or office**. Wayne Grudem observes, "The word *apostle* can be used in a broad or narrow sense. In a broad sense, it just means 'messenger' or 'pioneer missionary.' But in a narrow sense, the most common sense in the New Testament, it refers to a specific office. . . . If any in modern times want to take the title 'apostle' to themselves, they immediately raise the suspicion that they may be motivated by inappropriate pride and desires for self-exaltation, along with excessive ambition and a desire for much more authority in the church than any one person should rightfully have."[4]

The word *apostle*, in its broad sense, refers to those gifted by the Holy Spirit to start new churches and missions. True apostles (i.e., church-planters) serve as solo leaders *only temporarily*. They follow God's call to start new churches from scratch, and they see it as their responsibility to develop and raise up other elders to serve alongside them as quickly as God allows.

MODEL #2: THE ECCLESIASTICAL HIERARCHY MODEL

The second faulty model of leadership is the ecclesiastical hierarchy model. In this model there is a hierarchy of leadership, from deacon all the way up to bishop, cardinal, or even pope. A local church's leaders are not shepherds selected from *within* the flock, but outsiders brought in to serve for a season before moving on to serve somewhere else. Additionally, the higher offices of leadership such as bishop and cardinal usually don't pastor a specific flock, but rather serve as "leaders at large."

Again, there are a number of problems with this model biblically.

1. **The words *bishop* (overseer), *elder*, and *pastor* all refer in Scripture to the same office.** There is no biblical justification for using these terms to refer to different levels of leadership. A pastor is a bishop. A bishop is a pastor. Bishops are not "over" pastors, nor is any one bishop (i.e., the bishop of Rome) given more authority than any other.

2. **The Bible sees elders as part of the flock, not separate from it.** "Be on guard for yourselves and for all the flock, *among which* the Holy Spirit has made you overseers" (Acts 20:28). An elder is both a shepherd and a sheep. He is part of the flock, and he is entrusted by God to watch over it.

3. **Elders are to serve in a particular local church.** Paul and Barnabas "appointed elders for them in every church and, with prayer and fasting they committed them to the Lord, in whom they had believed" (Acts 14:23). Likewise, Paul instructed Timothy to "put what remained into order and appoint elders in every town" (Titus 1:5). Elders exercise oversight of *a particular local church*. There is no such thing as an elder who has no specific flock.

In addition to the biblical problems with the ecclesiastical hierarchy model, it can create significant practical chaos. Wolves, heretics, and false teachers who rise to the ranks of higher leadership are able to exert their will over helpless Christians who are seeking to be faithful to Jesus and to the Bible. This scenario has played out over and over again in traditional Protestant denominations, many of which have abandoned biblical convictions despite the protests of the faithful people within their rank-and-file membership.

During the Reformation, John Calvin argued strongly that if pastors do not arise from and serve in a local church, they are not biblical elders.

Lesson 2: A Biblical Approach to Church Leadership 27

"It is a wicked spoliation of the church to force upon any people a bishop whom they have not desired or have not at least approved with free voice," he wrote.[5] "Ridiculous are those who wish . . . to be *called* lawful pastors of the church, and yet do not wish to *be* such! Natural sense itself . . . repudiates the notion that he who has never seen a sheep of his flock is the shepherd of it."[6]

MODEL #3: THE CEO/BOARD MODEL

The third faulty model of leadership is the CEO/Board Model. In this model, which closely mirrors corporate governance, the pastor functions as the CEO or "point leader" of the church. The elders are not seen as pastors, but rather as a sort of "governing board" whose job is to keep the pastors in check and provide a system of checks and balances (lest the ministry staff or pastors have too much power).

This model of church leadership persists even in many churches that agree (on paper) with the biblical teaching on eldership. But as Alexander Strauch observes, "the contemporary, church-board concept of eldership is *irreconcilably at odds* with the New Testament definition of eldership" (emphasis mine).[7] It is crucial that we reject the "church board" model of eldership just as resolutely as we reject the other faulty models of leadership. Churches that practice this model are not following the Bible's teaching on church leadership.

CONCLUSION

This resource is designed to help reform our practices of church leadership. And reformation requires us to identify where we've been wrongly formed, and allow the Scriptures to deconstruct and reconstruct our ways of thinking and living. The fact that the Holy Spirit can work through faulty models of church leadership does not make it okay for us to replicate those models. Jesus is the head of the church. And Jesus has taught us how he wants his church to be led. Our job is to follow his blueprint.

Here's the good news: God loves us no more when we follow his rules and no less when we don't! We are not saved by our rule-keeping, but by the substitutionary sacrifice of Jesus on the cross. Because Jesus has died and risen again for us, we're free to acknowledge where we've fallen short. We're free to tell it like it is. We're free to identify where our church leadership structures are flawed and faulty and unhealthy. And we're free to change those structures—not just to "get things right," but to enter more deeply into the joy of our Father, and to better honor and glorify our great Lord and Savior.

DISCUSSION QUESTIONS

1. What do you perceive are some challenges of leading in plurality? What are the benefits?
2. Share about a time when you mistook your personal ambition for God's "calling." What did you learn in the process? How has it changed the way you discern God's calling?
3. Identify other vocations where qualifications really matter. What are the dangers of unqualified people in these vocations? Likewise, what are the dangers of unqualified elders in the church?
4. What's most compelling to you about the biblical model of church leadership? Why?
5. Which of the three flawed models of church leadership have you personally experienced? What strengths and weaknesses did you observe in that model?
6. What further questions does this lesson raise for you?

lesson

EXERCISE

2

FALSE RIGHTEOUSNESS

For Christ is the end of the law for righteousness to everyone who believes. (Romans 10:4)

Spiritual leadership is a dangerous undertaking. Leaders usually rise to leadership because of God's gifting, calling, and empowerment. But once there, they can easily develop a subtle sense of self-righteousness that communicates, "I'm here because I *deserve* to be here." This prideful self-dependence has brought God's judgment on many leaders in the Old Testament, as well as today.

One of the most indispensable tools of healthy spiritual leadership, then, is keen sense of "gospel self-awareness." Every leader must know the answer to the question, where will I tend to find my righteousness? When I'm not leaning on Jesus, what *will* I most likely be leaning on? To put the question another way—what do I count on to give me a sense of "leadership credibility"? Below are some common examples. Mark the one that best describes you.

- *Discipline Righteousness:* I work hard and have a strong sense of self-discipline; clearly I'm equipped to lead others.
- *Family Righteousness:* Because I "do things right" as a parent, I'm a better and more godly leader than those who have unruly kids.
- *Theological Righteousness:* I have good theology, therefore I'm obviously a credible spiritual leader.

- *Intellectual Righteousness:* I am better read, more articulate, and more culturally savvy than others, which makes me leadership material.
- *Accessibility Righteousness:* In a world that's busy, I'm always accessible and available to others when they need me.
- *Mercy Righteousness:* I care about the poor and disadvantaged the way *everyone* should. I'm not surprised that people look to me as a leader.
- *Legalistic Righteousness:* I obey God's commands. In our sin-warped culture, it's natural that younger Christians should look to me as a godly example.
- *Financial Righteousness:* I manage money wisely and stay out of debt. That proves my wisdom and trustworthiness as a leader.
- _____ *Righteousness:* [I'm godly, credible, "in the right" because…].

Once you've identified your most common source of counterfeit righteousness, reflect on how it colors your life and leadership.

- How does it cause you to feel superior to others who aren't "righteous" in this way?

- How does it hinder you from loving others?

- How does it keep you from deep dependence on the Holy Spirit?

- How does it work against humility and repentance?

The Bible is relentless about the contrast between works-righteousness (self-righteousness) and faith-righteousness. Wherever we find a sense of our own righteousness, we're not resting in the righteousness of Jesus. Therefore, to grow in the gospel and in our love for Christ, we must turn from self-righteousness. Consider Paul's own example of this in Philippians 3:

> If anyone else thinks he has reason for confidence in the flesh, I have more: circumcised on the eighth day, of the people of Israel, of the tribe of Benjamin, a Hebrew of Hebrews; as to the law, a Pharisee; as to zeal, a persecutor of the church; as to righteousness under the law, blameless. But whatever gain I had, I counted as loss for the sake of Christ. Indeed, I count everything as loss because of the surpassing worth of knowing Christ Jesus my Lord. For his sake I have suffered the loss of all things and count them as rubbish, in order that I may gain Christ and be found in him, not having a righteousness of my own that comes from the law, but that which comes through

faith in Christ, the righteousness from God that depends on faith. (Philippians 3:4b–9)

Follow Paul's example here by going through these steps:

1. *Identify* your reasons for confidence in the flesh. Whatever false source of righteousness you identified, you probably *are* strong in that area! List your strengths. Make clear the possible ways you could "boast" in this area.

2. *Turn from* these areas of confidence. Actually count them as loss. Reflect on how they fall short—how they cause you to look down on others, to be self-reliant, to boast in yourself rather than in Christ. In prayer, affirm before God that these areas of self-righteousness are "rubbish."

3. *Rest* in the righteousness of Jesus Christ. Embrace the promise of the gospel—that you are "in the right" because of Jesus's righteousness that has been credited to you by faith. Dwell on how much better, how much deeper, how much fuller "righteousness from God by faith" actually is, compared to your own "righteousness."

4. *Practice ongoing repentance* in this area. Daily, turn from your self-righteousness and rest again in the righteousness of Christ. Remember, your credibility and standing as a Christian and as a leader comes entirely from grace, not from works. Whatever good disciplines and qualities you *have* developed are evidences of God's grace, not fodder for comparing yourself to others. Enlist the help of your spouse or a close friend in this exercise.

3

THE PRIMACY OF CHARACTER

OBJECTIVE

To consider the biblical priority of character in spiritual leadership.

SCRIPTURE READING

- 1 Timothy 3:1–16; Titus 1:1–9

ARTICLE

We commonly refer to America as a democracy, but it might be more accurate to call it a *meritocracy*. We measure our worth based on what we've accomplished. We are a nation of achievers, eager to display our competence.

So it's natural for us, even when we approach the topic of eldership, to look for things to do. What do I need to accomplish? Where's the checklist? What book should I read? What doctrine should I study? What test do I need to pass? But this is exactly the *wrong* way to approach biblical eldership. Eldership is much less about competence than about *character*.

CHARACTER MATTERS MOST

The biblical criteria, or qualifications, for eldership are listed in 1 Timothy 3 and in Titus 1. The two lists are virtually identical, with a few differences. As you study these biblical texts, you'll see that about ninety percent of the qualifications are focused on a man's character. To qualify as an elder, a man must be above reproach, hospitable, temperate, devout, and so on.

However, character is evaluated subjectively, not objectively. There's no multiple-choice exam to determine whether you are "well thought of by outsiders" (1 Timothy 3:7). Instead, your character in that area can only be evaluated by asking outsiders (non-Christians) about you. If you don't have a good reputation with them, you don't qualify for eldership. It's that simple.

Therefore, any man who aspires to eldership must give himself to the formation of godly character. *The cultivation of Christlike character is essential to spiritual leadership.* And this is why the gospel is essential to spiritual leadership. Admitting the flaws and weaknesses in your character, and trusting God to transform them, is going to take a big view of God's grace and a firm grasp of your identity in Christ.

IDENTIFYING CHARACTER

Identifying behavioral sins is often relatively easy. Identifying character flaws is harder and more humbling. How can we begin to gain insight into who we are? How can we discern the contours of our character? Consider these four biblical realities:

- *Character is formed over time.* The English word *character* comes from a Greek and Latin term that describes the mark left by an engraving tool. It is how you have been etched, marked, formed. Christian philosopher Dallas Willard defines character as "who a person is and what they can be counted on to do."[1]

You don't just wake up one day and have godly character. The character you currently have has been formed over time, by small choices and decisions that have molded you and shaped your being. Therefore, discerning the nature of your character always involves paying attention to how you've been formed. Your family background, your spiritual history, your most formative events and relationships—these influences have led you to become a certain kind of person.

- *Character is discerned in community.* It's the people around you—the people in community with you—who are the best judges of your character. For this reason, you must invite others into the process of character discernment. And you should expect that a healthy church will not move you toward leadership until you have been in gospel-saturated community for a long time, really allowing others into the nitty-gritty details of your life and soul.

- *Character is best evaluated under pressure.* All of us can put on a good show when we have to. In fact, most of us are constantly striving to keep up appearances and look good to other people. As you assess your own character, don't look at how you act on your best day. Rather, consider what you're like under pressure: an exhausting day at work, an emotionally draining ministry situation, a fight with your spouse. And expect your church leaders to evaluate *that* you, not the "better version of yourself" that you sometimes put forward.

- *Character and wisdom usually go together.* People who have cultivated biblical wisdom—that sense of patient, keen insight and discernment into life—have usually also applied that wisdom to themselves, which in turn has led to the development of godly character. This is why Proverbs urges so strongly: "Get wisdom. Though it cost all you have, get understanding" (Proverbs 4:7 NIV).

CHANGING CHARACTER

Once you've discerned the kind of person you are, how do you change? What means has God provided to transform you into a different kind of person? Here are four basic means of grace:

- *Repentance.* There is no change without repentance. And repentance is not a one-and-done action step, but an ongoing discipline. This is why Martin Luther observed, "Our Lord and Master Jesus Christ, when He said 'Repent,' willed that the whole life of believers should be repentance."[2]

  Repentance means seeing and being humbled by our sin. It means facing up to the selfishness in our souls. It means turning to God for pardon, peace, and power. Whatever gaps you see in your character, whatever follies and flaws you identify in yourself—the first step is to repent and return to God.

- *Turning from Idols.* The deep sins in our character are always connected to idolatry—the treasuring of created things rather than the Creator. Real character change requires identifying the idols you're prone to serve and destroying and dismantling them through repentance and faith.

  This is not really a "second step" different from repentance, but a fuller and deeper expression of repentance. As your heart is delivered from the worship of idols, and as you live in more vital union with Christ through the Holy Spirit, you will find the fruit of the Spirit being manifested in your character more fully.

- *Worship.* Treasuring Christ is the obvious antidote to treasuring idols. Nothing destroys false worship like true worship. When we see the majesty, glory, greatness, and sufficiency of God, we are drawn out of ourselves and toward him. Cultivating a passionate, intense, vibrant worship—both privately and publicly—is one of the best ways to experience true and lasting change.

- *Spiritual Disciplines*. Forming godly character requires applying yourself diligently to the Scriptures (Bible reading and study); listening to the Holy Spirit (prayer); cultivating awareness of your heart and your characteristic sins (reflection); being quiet long enough to hear God's conviction (silence/solitude); applying specific biblical truth to your areas of struggle and weakness (meditation/memorization); and similar rhythms that flow from the faithful practice of spiritual disciplines. If you haven't built a consistent habitual practice of spiritual disciplines, you shouldn't expect to grow in godly character.

Character change takes time. It may take years or even decades to meet the biblical qualifications for eldership. Don't get impatient. The Lord is not "over there," waiting for you to hurry up and change. He's right here, with you. He's dwelling in you by his Spirit—convicting you of sin, empowering your repentance and faith, and making you more like his Son. Because Jesus loves you, he's more committed than you are to changing you! And because he loves his church, he's committed to making sure it has the best and most qualified leaders. So enjoy the journey. And enjoy *him* in the midst of the journey.

DISCUSSION QUESTIONS

1. "It's natural for us, when we approach the topic of eldership, to look for things to do." How have you seen this in yourself? Be specific.
2. "Character is formed over time." What's encouraging about this idea? What's discouraging about this? How has this been true in your own life? Share examples.
3. "Character is discerned in community." What do you think the people closest to you would identify about your character? What *have* they already identified, and how has it helped you to grow?
4. "Consider what you're like under pressure: an exhausting day at work, an emotionally draining ministry situation, a fight

with your spouse." What characteristic attitudes or actions do you see in yourself in these situations? What drives those behaviors?

5. "If you haven't built a consistent habitual practice of spiritual disciplines, you shouldn't expect to grow in godly character." Share honestly with your discussion group what your general practice of spiritual disciplines looks like. How well have you kept to this pattern over the past thirty days? Explain.

6. What further questions does this lesson raise for you?

IDENTIFYING IDOLS

Little children, keep yourselves from idols. (1 John 5:21)

An idol, in the words of D. Martyn Lloyd-Jones, is "anything in our lives that occupies the place that should be occupied by God alone. Anything that . . . is central in my life, anything that seems to me . . . essential. . . . An idol is anything by which I live and on which I depend, anything that . . . holds such a controlling position in my life that . . . it moves and rouses and attracts so much of my time and attention, my energy and money."[3]

PART 1: DIAGNOSTIC QUESTIONS

Below are some questions that will help you identify your idols. The goal isn't to answer *every* question, but to trust the Holy Spirit to use two or three of them to help you discern your particular idols. Pray and journal your answers to at least two questions that resonate with you.

- Early on, what do I want to make sure people know about me?
- What makes me feel successful or competent?
- Whose opinion do I really care about? Who can make my day with their affirmation, or crush me with their disapproval?
- What gives me a feeling of peace and security?
- What distracts me or bothers me when it's not "just right"?
- What do I worry about most? What consumes my idle thoughts?
- What feels constraining to me?
- What do I fantasize or daydream about?

PART 2: SOURCE IDOLS

In his book *Church Planter*, Darrin Patrick identifies four basic "source idols" that lie deep in our hearts.[4] Most of our more visible sins and "surface idols" are manifestations of one of these four core idolatries. Based on your answers above, which source idol seems to dominate the landscape of your heart?

What I Seek	The Price I'm Willing to Pay	My Greatest Nightmare	Others Often Feel...	I Often Feel...
Comfort *(privacy, lack of stress, freedom)*	Reduced Productivity	Stress, Demands	Hurt	Boredom
Approval *(affirmation, love, relationship)*	Less Independence	Rejection	Smothered	Cowardice
Control *(self-discipline, certainty, standards)*	Loneliness, Spontaneity	Uncertainty	Condemned	Worry
Power *(success, winning, influence)*	Burdened, Responsibility	Humiliation	Used	Anger

PART 3: REPENTANCE

Identifying our idols is helpful—but that alone doesn't change us. We are changed only as we *turn* from our idols and worship Jesus. Below are three tangible steps of repentance. Go through these steps in private prayer, and then share your insights with your group.

1. ***Name your idols****.* Speak to God, in prayer, specifically, about the idols you serve. "Father, I confess before you that I have worshiped the idol of _____ .
    I have sought it instead of seeking you. I have served it instead of serving you. I have allowed it to dominate my life and heart. Forgive me, for I have sinned."

2. ***Neuter your idols***. In prayer, stand back and get perspective on your idols.
    a. Identify how *weak* they are: "God, this idol cannot deliver what it promises. It fails me time and time again! It has not done for me what you have done."
    b. Identify how *dangerous* they are: "God, this idol has enslaved me. It exerts influence and mastery over me. It wants to destroy me. And the longer I serve it, the more deeply it grips me."
    c. Identify how *offensive* they are: "God, when I serve this idol, I spit in your face and tell you that you are not enough. I dishonor my Savior and his sacrifice for me on the cross. Despite all you've done for me, this idol is more beautiful and fulfilling to me than you."
3. ***Replace your idols***. The way to replace your idols is to really appreciate, rejoice, and rest in all that Jesus has done for you. Often our "rejoicing" is only skin deep; we're thankful that Jesus died for us, but we're more consumed with our weakness, our sin, our shame, and our failure. True repentance means *really* rejoicing in Jesus's unending grace toward us!

    So, right here and now, in prayer, meditate on the beauty of Jesus and thank him for the specific ways that he succeeds where your idols fail. For instance, "Jesus, you are my salvation and my righteousness. You are the only one who never fails me, who will never leave me, and who can truly satisfy me. The idol of _____
    promises me _____ ,
    but it fails to deliver. Thank you that you alone are the one who can give me that. Thanks for these specific promises in Scripture: [identify specific promises that counteract your idols]."

Again, be sure to share your insights with your group. After all, character is developed in community. Give your community the chance to assist in doing God's work in your life.

lesson

4

THE LEADERSHIP TRIANGLE

OBJECTIVE

To consider the interplay of character, competence, and compatibility in spiritual leadership.

SCRIPTURE READING

- Nehemiah 1–2, 4–5

As you read, note what you learn about Nehemiah's *character*, his *competence* as a leader, and his *compatibility* with the particular situation facing God's people.

ARTICLE

In our last lesson, we noted that *godly character* is the primary criteria for biblical eldership. In this lesson, we want to add an important caveat: Character is not the *only* criteria. There are many men who have excellent character and who still do not qualify to serve as elders in God's church. The reason is because they do not meet the biblical qualifications in the areas of *competence* and/or *compatibility*. The categories of character, competence, and compatibility form a "triangle" of biblical leadership qualifications.

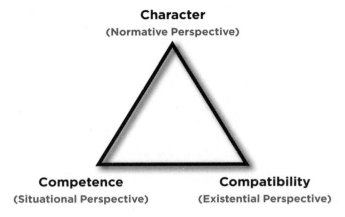

Character
(Normative Perspective)

Competence　　　　　**Compatibility**
(Situational Perspective)　　(Existential Perspective)

This "leadership triangle" is based on the Christian epistemology of Dr. John Frame[1] (whose contribution in this area is sometimes called *triperspectivalism*). Frame observes that the Bible reveals God's lordship through three lenses or perspectives. For God to be Lord means that he is in *control* of every situation; he is the ultimate *authority*; and he is *present* with his people (in both blessing and judgment).

Likewise, then, we can think about human leadership through these same three perspectives. A good human leader lives under God's *authority* (character); extends God's *control* by applying his Word to particular situations (competence); and manifests God's *presence* among his people (compatibility).

When we read the scriptural qualifications for eldership in 1 Timothy 3 and Titus 1, we can see that they fit neatly into this grid. A biblically qualified elder is one whose life and heart have been submitted to God and his Word (character), who is skilled in applying the truth of God to particular life situations (competence), and who ministers within a specific local context—people, church, mission, and city (compatibility).

Since we've already focused on character, let's now begin to examine the scriptural teaching about competence and compatibility.

COMPETENCE: IN LEADING THE HOME

The Bible requires that any potential elder be competent in the spiritual leadership of his home. This qualification is clearly stated in 1 Timothy 3:4–5 (NASB): "He must be one who manages his own household well, keeping his children under control with all dignity (but if a man does not know how to manage his own household, how will he take care of the church of God?)."

Notice the argument from lesser to greater: if a man can't pastor the little flock God has given him (his family), how will he pastor a bigger one (the church)? Therefore, men who qualify for eldership are men whose wives appreciate and respect their spiritual leadership in the home. They are men whose children love their dad and follow his leadership. They are not harsh or domineering toward their wives and children (1 Peter 3:7; Ephesians 6:4). They are men who can teach other men how to be godly husbands and fathers.

As a side note, this does not necessarily mean single men cannot be elders. Paul is simply acknowledging that most men have families, and the way to tell whether a man is a competent spiritual leader is to look at his family.

COMPETENCE: IN APPLYING THE BIBLE

Likewise, the Bible requires that elders be competent in applying the Scriptures. We see this reiterated in both 1 Timothy and Titus:

- "able to teach" (1 Timothy 3:2)
- "holding fast the faithful word which is in accordance with the teaching, so that he will be able both to exhort in sound doctrine and to refute those who contradict" (Titus 1:9 NASB)

Elders know their way around the Scriptures. They are able to counsel, disciple, and evangelize people using Scripture. Take note of some of the implications of the Bible's teaching about biblical competency:

- Elders must be able to "refute those who contradict." This implies a knowledge of opposing worldviews, and some basic skill in apologetics.
- Elders must "exhort in sound doctrine," implying a pastoral wisdom in applying Scripture to specific instances of unbelief, doubt, and disobedience.
- Elders must be "able to teach," implying that they can help others learn the Bible. The emphasis is not on their knowledge of Scripture, but their ability to impart it to others in accessible and understandable ways.
- When we combine the competence requirement of "able to teach" with the character requirement of "hospitable," we can see that elders must be competent missionaries. They must be able to winsomely and charitably teach and reason about the Bible with non-Christians, skeptics, and sojourners, as Paul did in Athens (Acts 17:16–34).

COMPATIBILITY: PHILOSOPHY OF MINISTRY

Compatibility is an element of elder qualification that is often overlooked, but it's no less important. Consider the implications of these verses:

- "It is a trustworthy statement: if any man aspires to the office of overseer, it is a fine work he desires to do" (1 Timothy 3:1 NASB).
- "Shepherd the flock of God among you, exercising oversight not under compulsion, but voluntarily" (1 Peter 5:2 NASB).

A man doesn't aspire to the office of eldership in the abstract—he aspires to the office of elder *in a particular local church*. If he is to fulfill his charge "not under compulsion, but voluntarily," he must be in alignment with the specific mission, vision, and direction of that church. In other words, he must be *compatible*. He must feel a sense of excitement about his specific local church and the ministry philosophy it has adopted. A lack of compatibility will bring tension and division, preventing unity and brotherhood among the elders. David Fairchild observes:

> An individual may possess the necessary knowledge/skill and have a tremendous heart and love for Christ, [yet] not be appropriate for a particular context. . . . There are a number of things to disagree about in the ministry and I believe it is perfectly healthy to do so. However, when it comes to the vision, values and mission of the ministry and the ways in which a particular local church has chosen to exercise her call, a person who does not believe in the church's philosophy of ministry will constantly need to be "talked into it" rather than moving forward together.[2]

COMPETENCE, COMPATIBILITY, AND THE GOSPEL

Proper competence and ministry compatibility are *biblical qualifications* for eldership. They are not optional! And the gospel frees us to honestly identify our deficiencies in these areas.

The gospel reminds us that God does not accept us based on our competence and compatibility, but solely on the merits of Jesus Christ. Because we are prone to find our identity in what we *do*, we can easily feel that not being qualified to *do* something (like become an elder) means that we are not acceptable as persons. But we must not confuse acceptance (justification) with maturity (sanctification)! The least mature person is as accepted in Jesus as the most mature. This is the good news we must preach to ourselves continually. Then, confident in God's delight in us, we can humbly acknowledge our deficiencies and resolutely apply ourselves to further growth.

The gospel also reminds us that Jesus has given us the Holy Spirit in order to empower us for ministry! We are *guaranteed* to grow in competence and compatibility because of the work of the Spirit. Jesus promised that the Holy Spirit would guide us into all truth (John 16:13). He also promised that the Spirit would gift believers for ministry (Romans 12:7–11) and help them know what to say in particular situations (Mark 13:11). Wherever you currently lack competence or compatibility, the Spirit of God is present and available to fill up your lack and help you grow.

DISCUSSION QUESTIONS

1. If a man is a poor spiritual leader in the home, how might that color his leadership in the church? What "lesser to greater" principles do you see here?
2. If a man is a good leader, but lacks competence in the Bible, what might be the results for those he leads?
3. Most people would agree that godly character is a basic pre-requisite for eldership. Why do you think we often ignore the prerequisite of *compatibility*?
4. If an elder has to constantly be "talked into" some aspect of a church's philosophy of ministry (small groups, worship style, etc), how might this affect the sense of "team" and chemistry among the elders? How might this also affect the entire church?
5. Why is the distinction between justification and sanctification important, in order for us to admit weakness and pursue growth?
6. What further questions does this lesson raise for you?

lesson

EXERCISE

LEADERSHIP TRIANGLE SELF-ASSESSMENT

Any kind of development or growth always starts with an accurate "snapshot" of our current reality. This exercise is designed to help you self-assess your current strengths and weaknesses as a leader in the three areas of character, competence, and compatibility.

First, take the assessment yourself. Then be prepared to discuss your findings with your group.

PART 1: CHARACTER

Rate yourself on a scale of 0–5 for each statement or question below. A rating of 0 means "this doesn't describe me at all"; a 5 means "this describes me perfectly." As you do this, remember: Reality is your friend. You can't grow as a leader if you're not honest about where you are. So assess yourself honestly and humbly.

_____ I practice consistent repentance and faith.

_____ I am aware of my own characteristic sins and heart idols, and I am seeking gospel transformation in these areas.

_____ I am aware of my "blind spots"—places of weakness in my character that I can only see with the help of others.

_____ I have no hidden sins or protected areas of darkness in my life.

_____ There are Christians who know the real truth about me and are helping me grow in Christlikeness.

_____ I have a genuine and growing love for Jesus and for others.

_____ People who know me well would describe me as patient, gracious, and self-controlled in conflict—not quarrelsome or short-tempered.

_____ I have personal friendships with non-Christians, and I am living a missionary life among them—praying for them, practicing hospitality, inviting them into community, etc.

_____ My spouse respects and responds to my spiritual leadership.

_____ I would feel comfortable telling a younger Christian to "follow me as I follow Christ."

_____ If someone spent a day alone with me, they wouldn't find anything surprising.

_____ If someone talked to my non-Christian friends or work associates, they would discover nothing that brings shame or dishonor on Christ or his church.

_____ If someone observed my marriage, they would see healthy patterns of communication, sexual intimacy, parenting, and headship/submission.

_____ I am above reproach in my sexual life, including freedom from pornography and/or fantasy.

_____ I consistently practice basic spiritual disciplines (Bible reading, prayer, Sabbath, solitude, etc.).

TOTAL SCORE: CHARACTER (out of 75 possible) _____

Go back and circle your highest and lowest score in this section.

PART 2: COMPETENCE

Again, rate yourself on a scale of 0–5 for each statement or question below. A rating of 0 means "this doesn't describe me at all"; a 5 means "this describes me perfectly." As you do this, remember: Reality is your friend. You can't grow as a leader if you're not honest about where you are. So assess yourself honestly and humbly.

BIBLICAL COMPETENCE

_____ I feel "at home" in the Bible—I can find passages quickly; I know major themes; I feel a general sense of familiarity with my Bible.

_____ I have read through the entire Bible.

_____ I can conversationally talk through the storyline of redemptive history without resorting to notes or study materials.

_____ I can place books of the Bible in their appropriate categories (minor prophets, historical books, wisdom literature, epistles, etc.).

_____ I can competently study a passage inductively—observing it, interpreting it, and applying it to my life.

_____ I know (off the top of my head) where to take someone in the Bible to establish the major doctrines of the Christian faith (sinfulness of humanity, deity of Christ, salvation by grace, the Trinity, etc.).

_____ I feel comfortable leading others in studying the Bible.

_____ I can quote important passages of Scripture from memory.

THEOLOGICAL COMPETENCE

_____ I am confident in my ability to clearly explain the gospel to someone.

_____ I have read a systematic theology book and/or have taken a systematic theology class.

_____ I understand basic theological vocabulary—words like soteriology, Christology, and eschatology are not strange to me.

_____ I understand regeneration, justification, and sanctification, and could explain them to someone else.

_____ I can describe the basic contours of important theological debates (Catholic vs. Protestant views of salvation, complementarianism vs. egalitarianism, Calvinism vs. Arminianism, etc.).

_____ I am able to confidently and humbly engage with a Mormon, Jehovah's Witness, or Muslim, and witness to them about Jesus from the Scriptures.

PRACTICAL LEADERSHIP COMPETENCE

_____ I feel confident to disciple someone.

_____ I feel confident to help others apply the gospel to their specific heart idols.

_____ I am aware of my spiritual gifting and how I function best in God's mission.

_____ I am able to confront sin lovingly and directly.

_____ People seem to respond to my leadership in small-group discussions.

_____ People seem to be helped by my counseling and encouragement.

_____ People often come to me for help in understanding and applying the Bible.

_____ I effectively train, empower, and delegate to others in order to develop their leadership skills.

TOTAL SCORE: COMPETENCE (out of 110 possible) _____

Go back and circle your highest and lowest score in this section.

PART 3: COMPATIBILITY

Once more, rate yourself on a scale of 0–5 for each statement or question below. A rating of 0 means "this doesn't describe me at all"; a 5 means "this describes me perfectly." As you do this, remember: Reality is your friend. You can't grow as a leader if you're not honest about where you are. So assess yourself honestly and humbly.

_____ I am familiar with the mission, vision, and values of our church.

_____ I could articulate the mission, vision, and values of my church to someone who didn't know them.

_____ I feel "at home" in my church; I have a sense of ownership and personal concern for its overall health.

_____ I interact with a spirit of charity and partnership toward other biblical churches in my city, but I also feel a healthy sense of joy and excitement about what God is doing through my church.

_____ I feel "at home" in our theological convictions—this is what *I* believe, not just what my church believes.

_____ I have a general familiarity with the various "categories" and influences within evangelical Christianity.

_____ I have arrived at settled biblical convictions on some of the key theological issues of our time (eldership, divorce, homosexuality, authority of Scripture, etc.).

_____ I feel a sense of stewardship toward my city. I feel personally responsible before God for its welfare.

_____ I feel a sense of stewardship toward my church. I feel personally responsible before God to use my gifts to strengthen this local church and move its mission forward.

_____ I am faithfully involved in the life and ministry of my church. If I dropped off the grid, people and ministries would feel my absence.

_____ I am giving generously to my church.

_____ I deeply respect and submit to the elders/pastors of my church, while also realizing that they are imperfect human leaders who need to grow in the gospel just as I do.

TOTAL SCORE: COMPATIBILITY (out of 60 possible) _____

Go back and circle your highest and lowest score in this section.

EVALUATING YOUR RESULTS

Which of the three broad areas (character, competence, compatibility) is your weakest? Why do you say that?

What do your three lowest scores reveal about your need for growth?

What do your three highest scores reveal about the strengths you may bring to a team? Where are you using those strengths right now, and how might you use them in the future?

Again, share your highest and lowest scores with your group and invite feedback. Are you seeing yourself rightly? Do others affirm your strengths and weaknesses in these areas? And how can you address both your weaknesses and your "blind spots"?

INTERLUDE:
THE DUTIES OF ELDERS

Now that we've laid some basic theological groundwork for who elders *are*, we're ready to look at what elders *do*. We could summarize the biblical duties of elders in numerous ways. Rather than inventing my own categories, I've chosen to follow Alexander Strauch's basic outline, from his book *Biblical Eldership*. In this classic book he summarizes the responsibilities of eldership as *protecting, leading, feeding,* and *caring for* God's flock.[1]

From the outset, let's be honest: Shepherd language doesn't resonate with us today. I've never met a shepherd. Shepherding isn't part of our cultural heritage, and when we hear the Bible talk about "shepherding the flock," we don't come alive with vision and excitement. Personally, I get more excited about terms like "missional leadership" or "spiritual formation." Back in the early days of our church, when I was young and idealistic, I referred to myself as a "cultural architect."

Yet the Bible is relentless about this language of shepherding. The Psalms refer to God as our shepherd (Psalm 23:1). The prophets refer to Israel's leaders as "the shepherds of Israel" (Ezekiel 34:2). Jesus is called the "chief Shepherd" (1 Peter 5:4). And Peter urges the elders to "shepherd the flock of God" (1 Peter 5:2). Rather than inventing new terms that suit our cultural disposition, we're wiser to stick with the Bible's terminology and do the hard work of discerning how it speaks to our context.

Elders *are* shepherds of God's flock. We work for Jesus, the Chief Shepherd, who is returning to evaluate how we've done with his sheep (1 Peter 5:4; 2 Corinthians 5:10). That ought to fill you with awe and worship, and spur you to be painstakingly diligent in fulfilling your responsibilities.

So, following Strauch, we can summarize an elder's calling according to four basic categories:

- Elders *feed* God's flock: by treasuring *God's Word* and teaching it to others.
- Elders *lead* God's flock: by being *examples* in both character and skill.
- Elders *protect* God's flock: from false teachers and from spiritual apathy and sin.
- Elders *care for* God's flock: by *encouraging them in the gospel* through all kinds of life circumstances.

One other category that is implicit in the biblical text but often overlooked in modern scholarship is that elders are *missional*. They lead God's mission and train others to live as missionaries in their culture.

The rest of our study, therefore, will flesh out these five aspects of biblical eldership and how we can live them out more fully in our lives and ministry.

5

ELDERS FEED
THE CHURCH

OBJECTIVE

To better understand the importance of treasuring and being devoted to God's Word.

SCRIPTURE READING

- Titus 1:7–11; 2 Timothy 4:1–4; Jude 3–4

Consider especially the emphasis these texts place on sound doctrine.

ARTICLE

According to *Scientific American*, most human beings will starve to death after three to four weeks without food and water. Michael Peel, senior medical examiner at the Medical Foundation for the Care of Victims of Torture, notes that the longest known medically documented hunger strike lasted forty days.[1] To put it simply, without food, your body will die.

What's true of your physical body is true of the body of Christ as well. "I'm not getting fed at my current church" is a common cliché phrase among Christians, but it can often be true. Your city is littered with churches that no longer preach the gospel, believe the Scriptures, or delight in God and his glory. The people in those churches are spiritually malnourished. In fact, Scripture teaches that God judges unfaithful churches by causing them to starve for his word.

> "Behold, days are coming," declares the Lord GOD, "When I will send a famine on the land; not a famine for bread or a thirst for water, but rather for hearing the words of the LORD. People will stagger from sea to sea, and from the north even to the east; they will go to and fro to seek the word of the LORD, but they will not find it." (Amos 8:11–12 NASB)

Like a good father, God wants his children to be well-fed, "constantly nourished on the words of the faith and of the sound doctrine" (1 Timothy 4:6 NASB). That's why he charges elders to exhort others in sound doctrine, to preach the Word, to contend for the faith . . . in other words, *to feed the church.*

Throughout Scripture, God's Word is described as food for the soul.

> When Moses had finished speaking all these words to all Israel, he said to them, "Take to your heart all the words with which I am warning you today, which you shall command your sons to observe carefully, even all the words of this law. For it is not an idle word for you; indeed it is your life" (Deuteronomy 32:45–47 NASB).

> How sweet are Your words to my taste! Yes, sweeter than honey to my mouth! (Psalm 119:103 NASB)

> And he said to me, "Son of man, feed your belly with this scroll that I give you and fill your stomach with it." Then I ate it, and it was in my mouth as sweet as honey. And he said to me, "Son of man, go to the house of Israel and speak with my words to them." (Ezekiel 3:3–4)

> And the tempter came and said to Him, "If You are the Son of God, command that these stones become bread." But He answered and said, "It is written, 'MAN SHALL NOT LIVE ON

BREAD ALONE, BUT ON EVERY WORD THAT PROCEEDS OUT OF
THE MOUTH OF GOD.'" (Matthew 4:3–4 NASB)

Elders must be men of the Word. They must love, treasure, memorize, and meditate on the Scriptures. Like the first apostles, they must "devote [themselves] to prayer and to the ministry of the word" (Acts 6:4). And what makes an elder devoted to the Word is a deep awareness of his own need! A gospel-gripped elder knows how lost he is without the sanctifying, purifying, clarifying truth of God's Word. He knows how prone he is to lean on technique, experience, and intuition rather than on "the living and abiding word of God" (1 Peter 1:23). And he seeks the Spirit's renewing grace to continually awaken a deeper love for the Word.

As the Spirit renews our hearts, we increasingly become leaders who delight in God's Word—and who actually *use* it in every situation. As an elder, "if you . . . do your job faithfully, you are *praying* the Word, *preaching* the Word, *counseling* the Word, *singing* the Word, and *living* the Word."[2] Let's consider each of these in more detail.

Pray the Word. Elders are men mighty in prayer—and men whose prayers are saturated with the truth of Scripture. Prayer is often undervalued in our fast-paced, media-addicted, simplistic culture. And for that reason, it's perhaps the most vital spiritual discipline for mature leaders to develop. "Less mature Christians have little need to pray . . . there is no complexity to their worlds because the answers are simple."[3] But leaders who know the complexity of gospel ministry, the duplicity of their own hearts, and the inadequacy of their own resources are constantly being driven to prayer, and are finding in Scripture the words to give voice to their prayers.

Preach the Word. Not every elder preaches; but elders as a whole are responsible for the preaching ministry of the church. Therefore, every elder should care about preaching! And before you get up to preach the Word, you must allow it to preach to you. The best sermons come not just *from* a preacher, but *through* a preacher. "The audience does not hear a sermon, they hear a man."[4] If the preaching ministry in your church is shallow and felt-need oriented, if it's lifeless and academic, or if it just doesn't seem to be bearing fruit, the answer is to go to Christ in fresh repentance. Where is zeal for the Word lacking in *your* life?

Counsel the Word. Biblical pastoral counseling is different from giving moral advice or therapeutic psychologizing. Elders saturated in the Word may or may not have their Bible open in every counseling session. But they will be using the Bible all the time. They will "speak *of* [God] and *from* him, representing him to others . . . kneading the truth into lives. God comes at people directly and wants [us] to do the same."[5]

Sing the Word. In our day, we have delegated singing to "the professionals"—the worship musicians who lead our corporate gatherings. And certainly some people are more gifted musically than others! But singing is for all of God's people (Psalm 33:1; Revelation 15:3). Elders who are Bible-saturated and gospel-transformed will find psalms, hymns, and spiritual songs rising up in their hearts. Whether alone with a guitar or gathered with God's people, they will sing exuberantly and joyfully. They will be the lead worshipers in the church, pouring out their hearts and their songs to God in ways that others can see and hear.

Live the Word. As the Word of God takes root deeply in us, it begins to pour out of us not just in "formal" settings, but in all of our informal conversation and even in our internal dialogue. David Powlison reminds us,

> To be "filled with the Spirit" is to have your language alive to God, both your daily conversations with others and the inward conversation within your heart. Your cognitive stream-of-consciousness and your social interactions are meant to be psalm-like and psalm-informed. . . . A videotape of your outward speech and inward thoughts would look like a continuously updated and personalized psalm. The realities of a living relationship with Christ infuse the way you process the specifics of your daily life. You speak and think

new-minted re-creations and applications of Scripture into the exigencies of the moment, updated at every point by Jesus Christ.[6]

These reflections show the reciprocal relationship between feeding yourself and feeding the church—between spiritual discipline and sound doctrine. In order to keep a church grounded in the Word, the leaders must be men of the Word. Leaders who are lazy or lacking in their own spiritual disciplines will usually create churches that are long on style and short on substance—where methodology and pragmatism trump theology and formation. And such churches, despite the external appearance of success, usually produce spiritually malnourished people.

It's natural for discipline and desire to wax and wane throughout various seasons of life. Rare is the elder who is *always* resolute in the study of God's Word. Thus, the responsibility to *feed the church* is also an invitation to renewed repentance and faith on the part of the elder. Our passion for God's Word is not always what it should be, but our Father is waiting to pour out the Holy Spirit on weak men who run to a strong Christ! Let's look to him for fresh joy, renewed vigor, and deeper hunger for the truth of his Word.

DISCUSSION QUESTIONS

1. Which Scripture passage quoted in this article is most encouraging or challenging to you? Why?
2. "What makes an elder devoted to the Word is a deep awareness of his own need! A gospel-gripped elder knows how lost he is without the sanctifying, purifying, clarifying truth of God's word. He knows how prone he is to lean on technique, experience, and intuition." What other things, besides God's Word, do you lean on in ministry? Give specific recent examples.

3. When has the Word felt most "alive" in your life and ministry? Describe that season. What was joyful and fun about it?

4. Elders *pray* the Word, *preach* the Word, *counsel* the Word, *sing* the Word, and *live* the Word. In your own ministry, in which of these areas is the Word most absent right now? What do you sense the Lord provoking you to do about it?

5. What further questions does this lesson raise for you?

lesson

EXERCISE

THE GOSPEL AND SPIRITUAL DISCIPLINES

PART 1: PERSONAL REFLECTION

Use the questions below to honestly and thoughtfully assess your practice of reading, studying, and meditating on the Bible. Record your answers in a journal or in this workbook.

Reading

- What is your current practice of Bible reading?
- Do you use a daily Bible reading plan?
- How many times have you read through the entire Bible?
- How do you ensure disciplined time in your daily schedule for Bible reading?

Study

- What is your current practice of *studying* the Bible in a more focused, academic way?
- What tools do you use for Bible study?
- How do you choose what passages to study more deeply?

Meditation

- How do you practice Scripture meditation and memorization?
- What techniques or practices do you use to slow your mind and heart down in order to meditate on Scripture?

What are the most common hindrances in your life to reading, studying, and meditating on the Bible? What kind of help do you need to overcome those hindrances?

Use the questions below to honestly and thoughtfully assess your prayer life.

- What do you do intentionally in order to build the discipline of prayer into your everyday life?
- How often do you gather with others for the express purpose of prayer?
- How often do you set aside extended times of prayerful solitude and reflection?
- What does your prayer life with your wife and family look like?
- How do you keep track of prayer requests, answers to prayer, and evidences of God's grace in your life?

What are the most common hindrances in your life to a consistent discipline of prayer? What kind of help do you need to overcome those hindrances?

PART 2: GOSPEL APPLICATION

What obvious weaknesses did this exercise surface?

What heart-sins might lie underneath these weaknesses? (Here are some possibilities: self-sufficiency, self-reliance, laziness, apathy, greed, comparison, control, etc.)

How do you tend to minimize or ignore these weaknesses and heart sins? How does this keep you from really engaging and enjoying God's Word?

What would it mean for you to bring these weaknesses and heart sins before Jesus? What do you need to ask for and receive from him? How does he promise to receive you and change you?

Repent and Believe. Take a moment to confess in prayer the sin, unbelief, and selfishness that lie behind your hindrances. Then feast your mind on the promises of the gospel and invite the Holy Spirit to transform you. Commit to one new or renewed discipline—with God's help. Share this with your group or mentoring elder for accountability.

6

ELDERS LEAD
THE CHURCH

OBJECTIVE

To better understand the spiritual dynamics of leadership, and to grow in character and skill through believing and applying the gospel.

SCRIPTURE READING

- Psalm 78

ARTICLE

> Skillful shepherds will lead the sheep. They will not be content for the flock to remain as they are, nor even to manage them more efficiently. They will seek the growth of the flock numerically. They will also seek their progress, individually and corporately, towards maturity. They will not be managers, for managers deal in seen realities, but leaders, for leaders deal in unseen potentials.
>
> — Derek Tidball, *Skillful Shepherds*[1]

We saw in our last lesson that elders are to *feed* the flock. But just as crucial—and perhaps even more challenging—they are responsible to *lead* the flock. Leadership is tough because it can't be forced or faked. As J. Oswald Sanders says, "Spiritual leaders are not made by election or appointment. . . . Simply holding a position does not make one a leader, nor do taking courses in leadership or resolving to become a leader. . . . Spiritual leadership is a thing of the Spirit and is conferred by God alone."[2]

One of the most notable spiritual leaders in all the Bible was King David. Psalm 78 recounts how God personally chose David "from among the sheep" and called him into leadership. The psalm ends by describing David's leadership this way: "David shepherded them with integrity of heart; with skillful hands he led them" (Psalm 78:72 NIV). This short summary captures two essential components of effective spiritual leadership.

"INTEGRITY OF HEART": EXEMPLARY CHARACTER

Elders are to lead the church by example (1 Peter 5:3). *The kind of men they are* is a crucial component of their leadership. Qualified elders have integrity of heart. They're not in it for the position, the title, or the prestige. They're in it because they love Jesus and are called by the Spirit to serve. In addition, they are the kind of men that other men want to emulate. They have a selflessness, a depth, and a substance to their character that lends weight and authority to their leadership.

Even non-Christian observers recognize the importance of character. Lord B. L. Montgomery wrote: "Leadership is the capacity and will to rally men and women to a common purpose, *and the character which inspires confidence*."[3] Dr. Leonard Sax, in his insightful book *Boys Adrift*, notes that boys become men by "[taking] their cues from the grown-ups they see around them . . . boys are looking for models of mature adulthood." In Sax's estimation, the cultural epidemic of unmotivated, underachieving young men is due in part to "the devaluation and dis-integration of the masculine ideal."[4] If boys do not have men of strong character to learn from, they will not become men of strong character themselves.

Elders must be men of strong character who lead by the force of their character. A good elder knows that he leads the flock well by leading himself well. He pays attention to the depth and strength of his inner life. He pursues self-awareness and relentlessly seeks sanctification in areas of weakness. He realizes that God's people will follow him based primarily on who he is, not what he says. He is compelled to say to people, Follow me as I follow Christ (1 Corinthians 11:1), and he strives to pay close attention to himself (1 Timothy 4:16) in order to ensure that he's providing a reliable model of Christian maturity.

People are always making judgments about your character, but rarely do they share those judgments with you. Therefore, you must develop the habit of asking for feedback. People will often feign submission to your leadership out of politeness or guilt. But their real estimation of you will generally come out during instances of conflict or tension. When you ask about sensitive areas, do they willingly respond? When you say hard things, do they listen and submit? When you press for decisive change, do they make those changes? If not, it may indicate that they do not respect your character. Your leadership is not "weighty" to them. Sometimes that's their problem. But often, the problem is *you*. God may be holding up a mirror to graciously reveal some weaknesses in your character. Are you willing to look?

"SKILLFUL HANDS": EXEMPLARY ABILITY

Elders must also have "skillful hands"—they must possess the skills necessary for effective leadership. Theological acumen is not enough. Depth of character is not enough. Alignment with your church's vision and mission is not enough. Unless a man has proven that he has the skill and ability to lead other leaders, he should not be leading as an elder in God's church.

By saying that elders must be skillful leaders, are we adding something to the biblical qualifications? Not at all. Remember, 1 Timothy 3:2 requires that an elder be "able to teach." This same phrase "able to teach" is also used in 2 Timothy 2:2: "What you have heard from me in the presence of many witnesses entrust to faithful men who will be *able to teach* others also." Commentators note the tight semantic relationship between these two passages and suggest that they mutually interpret one another. The "faithful men" that Paul mentions in 2 Timothy 2 are, primarily, the elders. And the "ability to teach" that Paul expects of elders is precisely the ability to raise up other men who "will be able to teach others also."

In other words, to be "able to teach" is *to be a disciple-maker*. An elder who is "able to teach" is an elder who passes on the faith to others. He makes disciples who make other disciples. If he doesn't do this, he's not qualified to be an elder.

Your church likely has a number of decent men who are growing in character and theology and who have aspirations toward eldership. Maybe you're one of those men. Until you have a spiritual lineage behind you—until you have "passed on" the faith to others who are passing it on to others—you are not yet ready for eldership. God's mission, after all, is to "go and make disciples" (Matthew 28:19). That's what you're here for. That's what Jesus expects. That's what the church is to be about. If you haven't done that, how will you teach others to do it? If it's not modeled in your life, how will it happen in your church?

EQUIPPING THE CHURCH

If being "able to teach" means "able to communicate biblical information," that's a relatively easy skill to develop. But if "able to teach" means "able to make disciples who make more disciples"—now you *really* need Jesus! Because you need *all sorts* of leadership skills to make that happen. You need to grow in prayer, discernment, counseling, spiritual formation, hospitality, conflict resolution, cultural analysis, delegation, and strategic planning, to name just a few.

You also need to equip and empower all kinds of other Christians around you to use *their* gifts to further the mission. This will especially require you to empower women to serve. A church that holds to biblical eldership but does not empower women will be seen as chauvinistic—and even worse, it will likely *be* chauvinistic.

Wise, godly, masculine elders create a church culture in which women thrive in their God-given gifting. When this happens, it's incredibly winsome and attractive to outsiders. Western culture assumes that any distinction in gender roles automatically leads to oppression or subjugation. But when the gospel is alive in a church, freeing both men and women to thrive as servant leaders, that church presents a compelling picture that challenges cultural presuppositions.

Equipping the church involves recognizing the gifts the Holy Spirit has given to others and finding places where those gifts can come alive for the benefit of all. The "where" and the "how" will vary depending on your model of ministry. In our church, gospel communities (small groups) are the starting point. As we see people ministering faithfully within the context of their gospel community, we invite them into other areas of service and ministry, following Jesus's principle that "one who is faithful in a very little is also faithful in much" (Luke 16:10). However your church equips and empowers people for ministry, it's the elders who are ultimately responsible to ensure that this work happens.

You don't have to be a super leader to equip the church effectively. All of us have different God-given gifts and talents. Some men are endowed with great natural ability, while others have more meager skills. But all of us can make disciples. All of us can pass on the faith. The Bible doesn't require you to be a visionary, apostolic, entrepreneurial genius. It *does* require you to be a faithful, obedient Christian who takes the Great Commission seriously and gives yourself wholeheartedly to it. The fruit of that in your life should be a heritage of disciples who are walking with Jesus and leading others because of your influence and investment.

CONCLUSION

We started this lesson looking at David. We observed that "integrity of heart" and "skillful hands" provide two summary categories for effective shepherding leadership. But we will miss the point unless we see Jesus as the "greater David"! Psalm 78 points us back to David as a way of pointing us forward to Jesus. And Jesus is our only hope for growing in integrity and skill.

Psalm 78:67–72 presents a somewhat "idealized" portrait of David. After all, didn't he commit adultery with Bathsheba? Didn't he murder Uriah? Didn't he fail in his leadership of his own son Absalom? For all his great moments, he had some colossal failures! And this is precisely why the psalmist is pointing us to David—because David is not just a model of leadership effectiveness; he's a model of trust and hope in God.

Psalm 78 (a psalm *about* David) must be read alongside Psalm 51 (a psalm *of* David). In Psalm 51 we see David cry out to God in weakness: "Have mercy on me, O God, according to your steadfast love" (Psalm 51:1). We see him plead with God for renewed integrity: "Create in me a clean heart, O God, and renew a right spirit within me" (Psalm 51:10). The writer of Psalm 78 isn't ignoring David's weaknesses in character and skill; rather, he counts David's response to these weaknesses as *part of* his integrity of heart. David is a model leader because he *knew* he was not a model leader. He spoke honestly of his sins and struggles, and sought the Lord for mercy, grace, and power.

There is only one leader in all the Bible who truly led with integrity of heart—who had "no deceit in his mouth" (Isaiah 53:9). And there's only one leader who had perfect skill: "A bruised reed he will not break, and a faintly burning wick he will not quench; he will faithfully bring forth justice" (Isaiah 42:3). Our hope is not in our integrity and skill, but in Jesus's integrity and skill. As we look to Jesus, and point others to him through our leadership, we will find ourselves both humbled (so that we can honestly admit the gaps in our character and skill) and strengthened (so that we can earnestly pursue growth in character and skill).

DISCUSSION QUESTIONS

1. "Managers deal in seen realities . . . leaders deal in unseen potentials." How does this change your thinking about leadership?
2. "Elders . . . are [to be] the kind of men that other men want to be like." Who are the men who have most exemplified godly leadership in your life? In what ways?
3. Whose example have you followed? What have you learned from him—perhaps even from his mistakes?
4. "People are always making judgments about your character, but rarely do they share those judgments with you. Therefore, you must develop the habit of asking for feedback." Practice this now with the men in your group. Invite them to speak honestly to you about what they see in your character, both good and bad.
5. Encouraging women to serve with their God-given gifts sounds obvious but can often be difficult in practice. Identify some women in your life whom you could ask about their experiences in church ministry and with elders. Ask them where they have felt encouraged and empowered in ministry and where they have felt discouraged and marginalized. Try to choose women with a variety of personalities, giftings, and life experiences (don't just ask your wife).
6. What further questions does this lesson raise for you?

lesson

EXERCISE

EXAMINING YOUR CHARACTER

PART 1: EXAMINING YOUR DISPOSITION

For a sports team to function effectively, each player must adequately assess his talent and know his unique role. The gifts and abilities that make a good quarterback are different from those that make a good defensive lineman. Furthermore, some players are endowed with great natural talent, while others must work hard just to earn a spot on the bench.

This same diversity applies in spiritual ministry. First Corinthians 12:4–6 says there are "varieties of gifts . . . varieties of service . . . and varieties of activities." Jesus implied in the parable of the talents (Matthew 25:14–30) that God entrusts his servants with different resources to manage. So in order for an elder team to work with maximum kingdom effectiveness, each elder must rightly assess his own gifts and those of the other elders, and be free from envy, pride, and selfishness.

One way to surface the yet-unsanctified areas in your own heart is to examine your disposition toward other leaders around you. Meditate on these questions and journal your answers:

- What other leaders in your church community do you sometimes find yourself comparing yourself to? Why? Under what circumstances?

- What gifts and abilities do those leaders have that you wish you had? Why?

- Where do you feel insecure—like you don't "measure up" to these other leaders? Where do you feel more skilled/competent/effective than them?

- In what ways do you catch yourself being critical or judgmental toward their ministry?

Go back over your answers. Notice that the questions, though phrased innocently, are simply intended to surface the sins of *pride* and *envy*. These are character defects that must be rooted out by repentance and gospel transformation.

A godly, mature Christian leader who is grounded in the gospel

- will not feel any sense of comparison or competition with other men who are gifted differently.
- will feel "at home" in how God has made him, with an accurate sense of who he is and how his gifts contribute to the mission.
- will celebrate how God uses others in ministry, rather than criticizing or judging their success.
- will be honest about weaknesses in his own character without excusing them by calling them issues of "personality" or "temperament."
- will be able to legitimately (with integrity of heart) look around the room and affirm God's providence in gifting other men more generously than himself.
- will be able to affirm God's gifting and calling of some elders to labor at preaching and teaching (and therefore receive support from the body), even though he knows their faults and sins and weaknesses.

As you've done this exercise, what sins have you been convicted of?

How do you see Jesus living victoriously over these sins? Give specific examples from his life.

Since his victory is counted as yours, how does the gospel free you from your sin? How do you need to repent and believe so that you can work in humility and love with other elders?

PART 2: EXAMINING YOUR MARRIAGE AND SEXUALITY

Sexual sin is by far the leading cause of disqualification among Christian leaders. You can expect temptation in this area to increase if you aspire to eldership, as Satan will seek to discredit the gospel by ruining you.

Your assignment for this lesson, therefore, is to sit down with your wife (if you're married) and talk through your marital and sexual issues honestly. Everyone has marital frustrations. Do not give in to the temptation to hide them. Talk about them with your wife, and then bring them into the light with your mentoring elder or group. Below are some questions to help. (If you're single, work through whichever questions apply to you.)

- What are the specific areas of tension, frustration, or temptation in your sexual life?

- Are there any sexual sins or struggles in your life that you're not talking about?

- Are you and your wife both satisfied with the frequency and quality of sex?

- What is your greatest fear or insecurity, sexually? What is your wife's?

- If you found yourself feeling attracted to someone else, what would you do?

- Sometimes marital difficulties require an outside advisor. Who are the "safe men" in your life whom your wife could go to if she needed help confronting you (and whom you would respect and listen to)? Who are the "safe women" whom your wife would listen to if you needed help in confronting her?

- How does your wife feel about your relationship with your children and your skills as a father?

- Has this exercise revealed a need for more focused counseling or healing in any specific area? Do you need to step back from the pursuit of eldership to allow for this?

When you have had this conversation, please have your wife sign and date this page in your notebook. If this exercise reveals a need for further mentoring or counseling, please talk with your mentoring elder immediately.

My husband and I have talked through these matters together.

_____   _____
[Wife's Signature]   [Date]

lesson

7

ELDERS PROTECT THE CHURCH

OBJECTIVE

To better understand false teachers and how to guard the church from them.

SCRIPTURE READING

- Jeremiah 27–28

ARTICLE

If there's one thing that kills the spiritual vitality of a church, it's false teaching. And if there's one thing we shouldn't be surprised by, it's the presence of false teaching. Paul told the elders at Ephesus to *expect* that men from their own number would rise up and distort the truth (see Acts 20:28–31). And the pastoral epistles—1 Timothy, 2 Timothy, and Titus—are full of admonitions to be on the lookout for false teachers. Elders are responsible to *protect* the church from wolves and false teachers. They do this by guarding their own hearts and by guarding sound doctrine.

GUARDING YOUR OWN HEART

See to it, brothers, that none of you has a sinful, unbelieving heart that turns away from the living God. But encourage one another daily, as long as it is called Today, so that none of you may be hardened by sin's deceitfulness. We have come to share in Christ if we hold firmly till the end the confidence we had at first. (Hebrews 3:12–14 NIV 1984)

The warning of Hebrews 3 is a sobering reminder that our hearts are "prone to wander." Sin's deceitful influence can cause us to become hardened and unbelieving. Perhaps this is why Paul urged Timothy, "Keep a close watch on *yourself* and on the teaching" (1 Timothy 4:16). As the revered English commentator Matthew Henry observed, "Those are not likely to be skillful or faithful keepers of the vineyards of others who do not keep their own."[1]

Therefore, a wise spiritual leader is self-aware. He knows where he's likely to be tempted. He's cognizant of his weaknesses and character flaws—what Richard Lovelace called one's "characteristic flesh."[2] He's committed, as John Owen counseled, to "finding out the subtleties, policies, and depths of any indwelling sin . . . to trace this serpent in all its turnings and windings; be able to say, at its most secret actings, 'This is your old way and course; I know what you aim at.'"[3] The wise leader is diligent not just to fight sin, but to practice the positive disciplines of prayer, meditation, solitude, and Scripture study that tune the heart toward God.

Those who aspire to eldership are bound to experience great discouragement, frustration, and spiritual attack. The well-known Puritan Richard Baxter wrote: "The tempter will make his first and sharpest attack on you. . . . He has long practiced fighting, neither against great nor small, comparatively, but against the shepherds, that he might scatter the flock. . . . Take heed then, for the enemy has a special eye on you. You are sure to have his most subtle insinuations, incessant solicitations and violent assaults."[4] Satan hates the mission of God. He is out to destroy you and your ministry. If he can make you the instrument of your own ruin, the destruction is even greater.

So how, practically, do you guard your own heart? Here are three tested strategies:

1. **Cultivate personal intimacy with God.** Nourish your soul in the Word. Spend unhurried time in prayer. *Plan it.* (It's not going to "just happen".) Set aside days on your calendar for solitude and silence and personal renewal. Practice spiritual disciplines that keep your soul refreshed with a sense of the love and glory of God. The greatest temptation of leadership is to exalt *doing* over *being*. Sure, good leaders get stuff done, but effective ministry is always an overflow of a heart aflame with love for God.

2. **Mortify sin, resolutely and relentlessly.** As John Owen wrote: "Since it is our duty to mortify sin (Romans 8:13) . . . we must be at work! He that is appointed to kill an enemy, if he leave striking before the other ceases living, does but half his work."[5] Pride manifests itself in a careless disposition toward sin, but humility brings with it a wary watchfulness. No matter how much progress you make in sanctification, you are always vulnerable. "Let him who thinks he stands take heed that he does not fall" (1 Corinthians 10:12 NASB). For practical help in putting sin to death, leaders would be wise to consult Owen's great treatise *The Mortification of Sin* and put its principles into practice.

3. **Create honest community.** Leadership is lonely. Because of the dangers posed by needy, divisive, or power-hungry people, spiritual leaders can easily isolate themselves from true community. They can focus on shepherding the flock and forget that they too are part of Jesus's flock. This is a tragic mistake. None of us can see our own faces. You need people around you who know you well and whom you can trust with the honest truth about yourself. You need a community who will encourage you in the gospel and help you see your own sin, unbelief, and idolatry. Creating this kind of community is difficult because you can't trust everyone. But it's critical, because

if you don't have it, you're isolated and vulnerable to spiritual attack. Don't make excuses. Figure it out.

GUARDING SOUND DOCTRINE

The word that's often translated "sound doctrine" in the New Testament is the Greek word *hugainos*, which literally means "healthy." When it's translated "sound," it has the connotation of the "soundness" of a ship's hull: solid, secure, no leaks. These linguistic connections help us get a sense of the subtle destructiveness of false teaching. False teaching is like cancer that attacks a healthy body; it starts out barely noticeable, but grows over time until it breeds disease and death. False teaching is like a small leak in a ship's hull; left untreated, it will eventually sink the boat.

It's often easy to spot the most grievous examples of false teaching. But as D. Martyn Lloyd-Jones observes, "The most dangerous person of all is the one who does not emphasize the right things."[6] That's why Paul charged the elders in Ephesus to "Be on guard for yourselves . . . be *on the alert*" (Acts 20:28, 31 NASB). The Greek verb used here has the sense of constant, ongoing vigilance. Elders are first of all to keep watch over their own souls and make sure they are rooted in sound doctrine. Additionally, they are to guard the church by aggressively and swiftly confronting false teachers, "rebuking those who contradict" (Titus 1:9).

Dealing with false teachers requires deep gospel wisdom and a keen sense of spiritual discernment. Elders must know when they are truly dealing with a "savage wolf" (Acts 20:29 NIV), and when they are merely facing an opponent who needs to be "gently instructed, in the hope that God will grant them repentance leading them to a knowledge of the truth" (2 Timothy 2:25 NIV). They must be able to discern the difference between properly refuting false teaching and being drawn into "foolish and stupid arguments" which are "unprofitable and useless" (2 Timothy 2:23; Titus 3:9 NIV).

How can potential elders grow in their ability to make these distinctions? First, every potential elder should study the Scriptures with the goal of "knowing the enemy"—in other words, learning what the Bible says about the motives, conduct, and strategies of false teachers. Second, every aspiring elder should learn to distinguish between *issues central to the gospel* and *issues peripheral to the gospel*. Issues central to the gospel are worth fighting for; peripheral issues may still engender charitable disagreement and debate, but aren't always worth fighting over.

We learn this distinction from the apostle Paul. Consider the following two Scriptures:

> It is true that some preach Christ out of envy and rivalry, but others out of goodwill. The latter do so in love, knowing that I am put here for the defense of the gospel. The former preach Christ out of selfish ambition, not sincerely, supposing that they can stir up trouble for me while I am in chains. But what does it matter? The important thing is that in every way, whether from false motives or true, Christ is preached. And because of this I rejoice. (Philippians 1:15–18 NIV 1984)

> When Peter came to Antioch, I opposed him to his face, because he was clearly in the wrong. Before certain men came from James, he used to eat with the Gentiles. But when they arrived, he began to draw back and separate himself from the Gentiles because he was afraid of those who belonged to the circumcision group. The other Jews joined him in his hypocrisy, so that by their hypocrisy even Barnabas was led astray.
>
> When I saw that they were not acting in line with the truth of the gospel, I said to Peter in front of them all, "You are a Jew, yet you live like a Gentile and not like a Jew. How is it, then, that you force Gentiles to follow Jewish customs?" (Galatians 2:11–14 NIV 1984)

Evidently the teachers in Philippi, though ministering from impure motives, were not corrupting the gospel. Though Paul clearly disagreed with them, he didn't engage them in debate, but rather took comfort in the more important fact that Christ was being proclaimed. However, in Galatia, Paul publicly confronted Peter because his behavior was "not in line with the truth of the gospel." Peter's favoritism toward Jewish Christians was confusing the gospel in the eyes of the Gentile believers, and therefore Paul rebuked him in the presence of all. The disagreement in Philippi was over an "open-handed" issue. The disagreement with Peter concerned a "closed-handed," centrality-of-the-gospel matter. It was worth fighting over.

CONCLUSION

The idea of guarding sound doctrine can easily be misunderstood as enforcing doctrinal conformity, as if the goal is for your whole church to be able to pass a doctrinal exam. But doctrine is not an end in itself; it is a means to an end. And the end is knowing and treasuring Jesus Christ! Sound doctrine gives people a clear vision of Jesus, so that they can know him more fully, trust him more boldly, and enjoy him more deeply.

Consider this observation from Richard Lovelace:

> Spiritual life flows out of union with Christ, not merely imitation of Christ. When the full dimensions of God's gracious provision in Christ are not clearly articulated in the church, faith cannot apprehend them, and the life of the church will suffer distortion and attenuation.... When any essential dimensions of what it means to be in Christ are obscured in the church's understanding, there is no guarantee that the people of God will strive toward and experience fullness of life.[7]

Lovelace's point here is profound. The Christian grows by faith, and faith needs truth for it to be laid hold of. When the "full dimensions" of God's grace in Christ are not clearly taught—through sound doctrine and good, robust biblical teaching—then faith is left with nothing to apprehend or lay hold of. As a result, the spiritual life of God's people will suffer.

Guarding sound doctrine, then, is about making sure people have truth to lay hold of. We care about doctrine because we want Christians to trust Jesus Christ more deeply and experience more of his power in their lives. So let's lead them by allowing good, healthy doctrine to unleash more of Jesus's transforming power in *our* lives!

DISCUSSION QUESTIONS

1. How does knowing the contours of your own heart and your own temptations help you in leading others? Why is this true?
2. "Those who aspire to eldership are bound to experience great discouragement, frustration, and spiritual attack." How have you experienced these things? Share and discuss.
3. When dealing with error, how can you discern whether you're dealing with a "savage wolf" (Acts 20:29 NIV), or whether you're dealing with someone who needs to be "gently instructed, in the hope that God will grant them repentance leading them to a knowledge of the truth" (2 Timothy 2:25 NIV)?
4. "Redemption is participatory, not imitative" (Lovelace). Reflect on this idea. This is one of the core distinctions between Protestant and Roman Catholic theology. If redemption is participatory, how does this heighten the importance of sound doctrine? Why is the teaching of sound doctrine necessary to the flourishing of the church?
5. What further questions does this lesson raise for you?

lesson

EXERCISE

THE GOSPEL AND CONFLICT RESOLUTION

Protecting the flock means consistently dealing with false teachers, unrepentant sinners, and difficult people—which inevitably leads to conflict. As the leaders and pacesetters for the church, it's crucial that elders are holy and healthy in conflict, neither passive and timid nor harsh and overbearing. This exercise is designed to help you assess your patterns in conflict and grow in confidence and humility.

Prayerfully reflect upon some recent instances of conflict with your spouse, and a "difficult person" you're ministering to. Circle phrases in the following list that apply to your conduct in these situations. Different words may apply in different circumstances.

LIST A

This must be confronted; it's a sin to ignore it.

This person just doesn't get it!

I'm right and they know it.

I wish they'd get their own life straight before judging mine.

I'm not letting this go!

They don't even have the facts straight.

I'm tempted to answer with sarcasm.

I feel my voice getting louder.

I will passionately argue my case.

This isn't over until we achieve full resolution.

LIST B

This isn't that important; it's not worth the effort.

This person isn't worth my time.

I'm not even going to get into this argument.

I wish I was somewhere else.

It's easier not to talk about it.

I'll just let it go.

I'm not deaf, I'm ignoring you!

This isn't going to get resolved, so why waste the time?

All of our failures in conflict ultimately come because we are man-centered, not God-centered. We are concerned primarily with *ourselves* (I want to be right; they're not respecting me; I shouldn't have to worry about this) or with the *other person* (what will they think of me; will I hurt their feelings; I don't want to offend them) instead of being concerned primarily with *God and his glory*.

Look back at the statements you've circled. How do they demonstrate a man-centered perspective? That is, how do they make you (or the other person) primary rather than making God primary?

Take some time to confess this as sin. The issue isn't just that your conflict-resolution skills need sharpening; the issue is that you have belittled God and His glory. How does Jesus's death for your sins free you from being consumed with yourself or others? How should this create both confidence and humility in you?

Think back through these instances of conflict. What would a radically God-centered approach to conflict look like? Write out the specific contrasts between your "normal" approach to conflict and a God-centered approach. (For example, instead of avoiding this person, I would move toward them in love because I want to see them honor Jesus.)

8

ELDERS CARE FOR THE CHURCH

OBJECTIVE

To better understand the nature of pastoral care (shepherding).

READING ASSIGNMENT

- 1 Peter 5:1–11

ARTICLE

As I sat down to write this lesson, I very acutely felt the weight of pastoring. Last week, a young woman in our church slept with her non-Christian boyfriend, then took the "morning after" pill. She is wracked with guilt and shame. A couple plagued by infertility finally got pregnant, only to experience a miscarriage. They are grieved and angry with God. A homosexually tempted man who recently came to know Jesus overdosed on crystal meth—for the second time this month. He is needy and confused. An older couple got a phone call that their twenty-something son had been thrown in jail on drug and alcohol charges. They are unsure how to respond. And this is just in the past seven days!

These real-life situations are the raw material for the work of shepherding. Elders are called by God to care for the flock. This means taking the big-picture truths of Scripture and working them into the fabric of daily life. What does it mean to believe and apply the gospel when a baby dies, or when I lose my job, or when my child is in trouble with the law, or when I feel trapped in patterns of habitual sin? "Pastoral work is simply bringing to full flower the bud of the gospel" in situations like these.[1]

Just as a medical doctor cures the body, the ancient theologians saw the work of the pastor as "the cure of souls." This analogy between physical medicine and spiritual medicine yields a number of helpful insights.

Manner. The best doctors have a good "bedside manner"—a warm, approachable disposition that puts the patient at ease. Likewise, good elders have a gracious spirit that breaks down defenses and creates an environment of hospitality, trust, and openness.

Method. Effective doctors always begin with accurate diagnosis. They don't just treat symptoms; they work to uncover the root of the disease. Likewise, effective shepherds work patiently to diagnose the root cause of spiritual maladies in the sheep instead of settling for surface-level solutions.

Goal. A good doctor is always aiming for wellness, wholeness, and health: The goal is a patient that is flourishing and free from disease. Pastoral care is after the same thing—on an even broader scale. We want to see people thriving physically, spiritually, psychologically, and emotionally, living in the "blessedness" that most fully displays God's design for humanity (Psalm 1:1–3).

Being an elder is like being a spiritual doctor. Elders patiently, lovingly care for the flock. Elders diagnose disease and treat illness. Elders celebrate health and encourage wellness. Elders apply the pastoral medicine of Scripture to the various sicknesses of the human soul. And they relentlessly, tirelessly labor to "present everyone mature in Christ" (Colossians 1:28).

Based on Colossians 1:28 and other Pauline texts, Derek Tidball summarizes Paul's approach to pastoral care this way (italics mine):

> Paul saw both the original proclamation of the gospel and its continuing proclamation in the church as one and the same process. . . . On occasions [his converts] ceased to be a joy and became, instead, a burden; but when that happened it was because *they had failed to appreciate the truth of the gospel to the full.* His pastoral approach was simply *to proclaim the gospel to them once more,* although this time *more thoroughly.*[2]

If Tidball is correct, we could summarize the nature of pastoral care as *gospeling the flock.* Our job is to help people *fully* and *thoroughly* believe and apply the gospel amidst the challenges and circumstances of everyday life.

The book of 1 Thessalonians provides a practical summary of the shape this "gospeling" work often takes in practice: "Admonish the unruly, encourage the fainthearted, help the weak, be patient with everyone" (1 Thessalonians 5:14 NASB).

- Some people are *unruly*—irresponsible, undisciplined, lazy. They need to be *admonished*: rebuked, confronted, warned.
- Other people are *fainthearted*—despondent, lacking faith. They need to be *encouraged.* The word literally means "to speak gently" and has connotations of consoling, comforting, strengthening.
- Still other sheep are *weak.* They need to be *helped.* The word here means "to hold fast" or "to cleave to" in a protective, caring sort of way.
- With all these types of people, *patience* is required—the kind of patience that only the Holy Spirit can produce.

PRACTICAL NECESSITIES OF PASTORAL CARE

Like good medical practice, good pastoral practice requires attention to the particulars. Pastoral care will be much more effective if elders work hard to develop a few key practices:

Being Present. We live in a busy, distracted culture that has forgotten how to honor people by simply being present with them. Cell phones ring during our meals. Text messages interrupt our conversations. Calendar alerts remind us of the next pressing engagement. In the midst of this frenzied world, a pastor who is *fully present* is a welcome foretaste of God's kingdom. Eugene Peterson observes: "The word *busy* is the symptom not of commitment but of betrayal. It is not devotion but defection. The adjective *busy* set as a modifier to *pastor* should sound to our ears like *adulterous* to characterize a wife or *embezzling* to describe a banker."[3] Good pastoral practice means being fully present with people, giving all of myself in their moment of need.

Listening. Listening is different than just hearing. Peterson describes listening.

> Pastoral listening requires unhurried leisure, even if it's only for five minutes. Leisure is a quality of spirit, not a quantity of time. Only in that ambiance of leisure do persons know they are listened to with absolute seriousness, treated with dignity and importance. . . . I must discard my compulsion to count, to compile the statistics that will justify my existence.[4]

Good pastors listen.

Praying. In our productivity-obsessed world, pastor-elders are prone to measure their effectiveness by what they get done. One thing that gets done very little is praying. But make no mistake: Prayer is perhaps the chief work of pastoral care. Praying with people and for people is an act of dependence, worship, and submission. It is also a deeply pastoral act. Prayer takes the moments of helplessness in people's lives—a car accident, a miscarriage, the loss of a job, the belligerence of a hard-hearted spouse—and turns them into moments of worship. In times when people most feel God's absence, prayer expresses our confidence in his presence.

Resting. God commands his people to rest. Not resting is *sin*. So don't justify your sin by labeling it "ministry." One of my pastor friends was mentored by an emergency room doctor who gave him some wise advice. He said, "There will always be a steady stream of sick and injured people. The need never goes away. So *you* must go away. You must have the discipline to go home, rest, and come back tomorrow."

The work of shepherding is exhausting and will wear down even the best men. "It is not the hard work or long hours that defeat a man; it is the emotional and spiritual stress . . . constant fighting among believers, complaints, unbelief, and disobedience ultimately wear down a Christian elder."[5] Effective pastors recognize that protecting their own times of rest—sleep, Sabbath, recreation, vacation—is vital to their ability to care well for the church.

Elders are charged by God to care for the flock. So be present. Listen. Pray. Rest. Like a good doctor, learn to apply the healing truth of the gospel to all types of spiritual malady. And realize that good pastoral care creates deep trust and confidence among the people you're shepherding. People will put up with mediocre preaching and leadership if they know they're cared for; but even the best preaching and leadership can't overcome a deficiency of care.

Most of all, remember that as you practice good pastoral care, you are projecting the image of Jesus Christ, the Great Shepherd of the sheep (Hebrews 13:20), who cares for his flock. He cares for his people *through* you.

DISCUSSION QUESTIONS

1. How does the analogy of a medical doctor help you in understanding the care of souls? What new insights do you gain from comparing the role of an elder to that of a doctor?
2. Good medicine is both *reactive* (responding to sickness) and *proactive* (promoting wellness). How do these same two categories apply to soul care and to leading the church? How can elders give adequate attention to both?
3. Being fully present, listening, praying, resting—which of these do you find most challenging, and why?
4. Why are good patterns of rest necessary for good pastoral care? What are your current patterns of rest? How can we help one another in this area?
5. What further questions does this lesson raise for you?

lesson

EXERCISE

IDENTIFYING PRIDE

Clothe yourselves, all of you, with humility toward one another.
(1 Peter 5:5)

The opposite of humility is pride. We commonly think of pride only as arrogance or haughtiness. But the essence of pride is *self-concern*. And self-concern can manifest itself either offensively (as arrogance) or defensively (as fear).

Below are two lists that show some characteristics of *arrogant pride* and *fearful pride*. Mark the characteristics you see reflected in your own leadership style. Then invite feedback from your spouse, and someone who has been under your leadership. (Note: This isn't an either/or exercise. Most leaders will display some tendencies of both.)

CHARACTERISTICS OF ARROGANT PRIDE

- Shuns genuine, peer accountability
- Tries to be in control
- Sees all issues as black and white; views people as either for or against him
- Threatened by people with legitimate differences; doesn't allow disagreement or critique
- Insensitive; doesn't take people's feelings into account as he leads
- Closed-minded; unaccepting of new ideas

- Sees other gifted, competent people as competition rather than partners
- Hypercritical of others
- Lacks self-awareness; unable to see his own sins, errors, and faults
- Cannot delegate genuine authority or significant positions to others
- Longs to be respected by everyone

CHARACTERISTICS OF FEARFUL PRIDE

- Unwilling to act unless he gains consensus from followers first
- Hesitant to take charge
- Sees all issues as shades of gray; reluctant to fight for anything
- Paralyzed by people with legitimate differences; always responding to disagreement or critique
- Overly sensitive; unwilling to hurt anyone's feelings
- Soft-minded; so welcoming of new ideas that error and heresy are tolerated
- Sees other gifted, competent people as threats
- Never critical of others—even when he should be
- Lacks self-confidence; paralyzed by awareness of his own sins, errors, and faults
- Wants everybody to have a voice in every decision
- Longs to be liked by everyone

After receiving feedback from your spouse and another person, look back at the characteristics you've identified and consider how the gospel applies to them.

- What biblical commands or imperatives does this characteristic violate?

- How are you avoiding the lordship of Jesus and/or the salvation of Jesus? That is, how are you trying to be your own lord and savior? What are you trying to control or avoid?

- How can the work of Jesus liberate you from the enslaving nature of these tendencies? If you were to really rest in Jesus and in his promises, how would it free you from these manifestations of pride? (List specific aspects of Jesus's work or specific gospel promises that apply here.)

- By faith, Jesus invites you to "put off" pride (through repentance) and "put on" humility (through dependence on the Spirit). Take time to pray and do that now. Then imagine and envision how a gospel-driven humility will look different in this area.

lesson

9

MISSIONAL ELDERSHIP

OBJECTIVE

To consider how our identity as God's missionary people informs our philosophy and practice of eldership.

SCRIPTURE READING

- Jeremiah 29; Acts 17

ARTICLE

Churches in the West are slowly beginning to awaken to the fact that Christendom—that is, the cultural predominance of Christianity in the Western world—is dead. As Peter Kreeft puts it, "[Many Christians act] as if we still lived in a Christian culture, a Christian civilization, a society that reinforced the Gospel. No. The honeymoon is over . . . [but] the news has not yet sunk in fully in many quarters."[1] As leaders wake up to this reality, they are rediscovering the missional paradigm of church leadership—a vision to lead the church as a countercultural, missionary entity rather than as a culturally favored institution. How should this impact our understanding of eldership?

Because we have grown so accustomed to reading the Bible through "Christendom lenses," almost all our thinking about eldership has focused on an elder's responsibility to *those already in the flock*. But what about those outside the flock? What about those who do not yet know Christ? God told Paul to keep preaching in Corinth because "I have many in this city who are my people" (Acts 18:10). Is that not true in your city as well? What is an elder's responsibility in leading the mission to the unchurched and dechurched people around him?

Existing books and resources on eldership have precious little to say about this question. They are so focused on the specific verses detailing an elder's responsibility to the church that they fail to answer the broader question *What is the church?* They miss the forest for the trees. If the church is a static, established institution, then perhaps elders should spend their time managing that institution—"running the church," as the phrase goes. But if the church is a missionary people, our fundamental understanding of eldership changes. The question *What is an elder?* cannot be answered unless we give attention to the broader question *What is the church?*

According to the Bible, the church is *God's missionary people.* God's called-and-sent ones. Throughout Scripture, God's pattern is to call people to himself and then send them out to display and declare his glory to the nations. The Greek New Testament word for church, *ekklesia,* replicates this pattern; it literally means "the called-out ones." And whom God calls out to himself, he sends on mission: "As the Father has sent me, even so I am sending you" (John 20:21); "*Go* therefore and make disciples of all nations" (Matthew 28:19). First Peter 2:9 captures this calling-and-sending dynamic in one verse: "But you are a chosen race, a royal priesthood, a holy nation, a people for his own possession,that you may proclaim the excellencies of him who called you out of darkness into his marvelous light." Notice that all four of the titles in the opening part of this verse capture the rich Old Testament imagery of God's calling and choosing a people for himself. The church is a people, not a place. God has chosen us and drawn us to himself so that we might proclaim his excellencies to those who don't yet worship him.

This understanding of the nature of the church is foundational to a proper vision of eldership. If the church is God's missionary people, then elders are missionary leaders. Elders are the chief missionaries, the missional pacesetters, of the church. If elders are living missionary lives, loving and serving non-Christians, the church will be doing so as well. If elders are failing in mission, the church will not be missional.

This focus on missional eldership is not a modern invention; it's a biblical qualification. First Timothy 3:2 requires elders to be "hospitable." This does not mean that elders must have church members over for dinner or publish their cell phone numbers on the church website. The Greek word used here is *philoxenos*, which literally means "the love of strangers." Hospitality is making a place for the stranger, the sojourner, the outsider. Therefore, an elder who is hospitable lives as a missionary.

What does this look like in actual practice?

An elder has a missional life. He does not call people to do what he himself is not doing. He practices missional rhythms in his own life. He knows and loves his neighbors. He has authentic friendships with non-Christians. He is praying for specific people and longing to see them come to know Jesus. He interacts normally and naturally with people outside the church.

An elder has a missional heart. He longs to see people know and follow Jesus. He sees worldly people not as enemies, but as spiritually lost people in bondage to sin and Satan—and he believes that God wants to reach them with the gospel. His love for Christ compels him to engage the culture. He is willing to get his hands dirty in the real messiness of people's lives. He has a "go to them" mindset instead of a "come to us" mindset. He is constantly wrestling with the tension of being in the world, but not of the world.

An elder has missional skill. He has developed competence and proficiency in sharing the gospel in all types of situations. He is aware of the basic types of unbelief and idolatry in the culture around him. He has a welcoming spirit toward self-righteous moralists, irreligious relativists, and everyone in between—and can talk about the gospel intelligently with all. He knows how to do basic apologetics; how to answer questions about the Bible; how to get underneath surface objections to heart-level issues of worship, trust, and obedience. He shares the gospel naturally and freely, not awkwardly and formally. He has learned all of this not by reading books, but by practice in actual situations.

An elder shapes a missional church culture. He realizes that it's not enough to be a missional person himself; he is responsible to lead a missional church. He is relentless about making sure that the church's culture—its "feel"—is hospitable toward non-Christians. His preaching, communication, and leadership always *assume* that skeptical people are present. He avoids us-them language, exalted "pious talk," and disrespectful or dismissive comments about outsiders. He shows charity and grace toward those who disagree. He engages the culture of his city so that he can speak the gospel intelligently to its cherished idols. He helps less mature Christians grow in the gospel so that they display deeply rooted love, grace, and hospitality toward non-Christians. He confronts religion, not just irreligion.

An elder leads the church toward cross-cultural mission. The Great Commission, by nature, is a "going" endeavor: "Go therefore and make disciples of all nations" (Matthew 28:19). Elders lead the church toward opportunities for cross-cultural mission that fit the energies, resources, and aptitudes God has placed within the body.

THE GOSPEL MOVES US OUT INTO MISSION

When the renewing grace of the gospel is at work in our hearts, it always moves us out into mission. When we are self-absorbed, apathetic, or unmotivated for mission, it's a sure sign that we have lost sight of the gospel. How could we not extend to others the grace that God himself has extended to us? How could we not pursue others as God has pursued us? Jesus is the ultimate missionary, who left the comfort of heaven and came to earth. He sought us when we were far from him—and he is still seeking those who are far from him.

If we find ourselves weak in mission, the answer is repentance and faith. We need to repent for our lack of joy! Our hearts have become disconnected from the beauty of the gospel and the majesty of salvation. As we turn, by faith, to rejoice again in the wonder of God's grace to us, we experience a fresh sense of the Holy Spirit's presence and power for mission. Mission is not something *we* are doing; it is something *God* is doing. And he invites us to join him in the joy of his kingdom work.

DISCUSSION QUESTIONS

1. What is an elder's responsibility in leading the mission to the unchurched and dechurched people around him? How can elders lead in mission while also caring for the flock? Discuss.

2. In our cultural moment, why is it crucial for church elders to have skill in basic apologetics? What will be the consequences for the church if elders cannot answer challenges to the faith intelligently and winsomely?

3. What does a missional culture in a church look like? Describe its basic contours. How would we know if we have one? What signs or markers should we look for?

4. Why should a greater apprehension of the gospel create greater joy in mission? How are you addressing the hindrances to mission in your own heart, and in the hearts of those you lead?

5. What further questions does this lesson raise for you?

lesson

EXERCISE

MISSION AND YOUR HEART

Any time the Bible commands us to "do" something, such as fulfill our mission, our sinful hearts tend to respond in either *legalism* or *license*. Look at the following lists and mark the phrases or thoughts you find yourself thinking as you wrestle with the call to missional living.

MISSIONAL RIGHTEOUSNESS

- I love non-Christians; why don't the people at my church love them like I do?
- Christians who aren't missional are immature and shallow.
- Others aren't as active in mercy and justice as I am.
- I'm *really* living in missional community; others are just talking about it.
- I share the gospel like crazy; why don't others do the same?
- Our church (or small group) is superior because we have messy, unchurched people showing up.
- Those Christians over there are lame; they aren't reaching out like we are.

MISSIONAL APATHY

- This "missional" talk is really nothing new; I'm doing fine.
- All this emphasis on "being missional" is legalistic; we're supposed to live in grace.
- God will bring people into my path if he wants to.

- I would like to be more missional, but my schedule won't allow it.
- My mission is greeting new people who come to church on Sunday.
- Too much focus on mission makes people worldly. It's better to avoid the culture than to be shaped by it.
- If having a "missional church" means we're going to have lesbians, drug addicts, and ex-cons showing up, I'm uncomfortable with that.

Your responses in the *missional righteousness* category reveal a tendency to justify yourself by your missional activity (legalism/self-righteousness). Your responses in the *missional apathy* category reveal a tendency to "turn the grace of God into licentiousness" (Jude 1:4 NASB) by falling into passivity and laziness. Run your answers through the following grid:

- What is God provoking you to do in the area of mission? List specific *objective commands* of Scripture as well as *subjective impressions* from the Holy Spirit as to how *you* need to more actively live on mission. (For "apathetic" responses, these will usually be ways of moving into mission more intentionally. For "righteous" responses, these may be things such as loving the Christians around you or repenting of the judgmental spirit you have toward other churches in your city.)

- What keeps you from doing this? What sinful attitudes and actions do you see in your heart that "short-circuit" the joy, love, and power of God, making mission a duty rather than a delight?

Now, apply the gospel.

HEAD: What do you *know* about Jesus's life, death, and resurrection? What specific biblical truths come to mind as you consider your own particular areas of sin and struggle?
   Example: Jesus is my righteousness. "For our sake he made him to be sin who knew no sin, so that in him we might become the righteousness of God" (2 Corinthians 5:21).

HEART: How do you need to *believe* this truth? If you really reckoned this as *true of you* because of your union with Christ, how would it change you?
   Example: When I really believe that my righteousness is in Jesus, I am freed from self-righteousness. Rather than comparing others' "missionality" to my own, I am free to love them and help them learn to live on mission.

HANDS: What do you need to *do* as a result? If God's Word is true (head), and if the gospel is true (heart), how will it be manifested in your actions?

> *Example:* Rather than judging other churches in my city that seem less missionally minded, I will begin to intentionally pray that God will bring renewal to them. With God's help, I commit to pray every time I drive by XYZ Church.

lesson

10

THE TEMPTATIONS OF LEADERSHIP

OBJECTIVE

To consider some peculiar dangers and temptations that leaders face.

SCRIPTURE READING

- Acts 20:29–35; 1 Samuel 15; 2 Samuel 11–12

Pay attention to how both Saul and David use their position of authority as an "excuse" to disobey God.

ARTICLE

Temptation is different than fantasy. Fantasy tends to operate in a dream world. Fantasy is about envisioning something you usually have neither the skill nor the opportunity to do. You may fantasize about taunting your opponent after scoring a touchdown in the Super Bowl, being one of the first humans to live on Mars, or about stealing top-secret government secrets from the Chinese. But you are not *tempted* to do any of these things. Temptation operates in the world of the possible. We are tempted by things we actually *could* do. That's what makes temptation . . . tempting.

This means that temptation is often situational. When we are in a situation where we *could* get away with something, we tend to face stronger temptation in that area. Therefore, leadership brings with it some peculiar dangers. Leaders, by virtue of their position, need to be on the lookout for five subtle but sinister seductions.

The seduction of entitlement. A position of authority always brings with it the danger of entitlement. Entitlement says "I shouldn't have to do X" or "I have a right to Y." It could be as simple as "I'm entitled to a good parking spot," or as complex as "I have a right to be respected." Entitlement always reflects a subtle works-righteousness: "Since I've done *this*, God owes me *that* (or God's people owe me that)." It's possible even to feel entitled to eldership: "After all I've done to serve this church, I have a right to be an elder." Rather than being awed by the gospel of grace and humbled by the opportunity to serve Christ, entitled people are focused on their own merits and desires.

Reflection Question: As a leader, what do you feel entitled to?

The seduction of comfort. A life of leadership in the church is a life of sacrifice. But for many of us who have been raised in a prosperous culture, sacrifice is not a welcome idea. Leaders are perpetually tempted by the allure of comfort. This can take many forms: the comfort of a stable church, the comfort of a generous budget, the comfort of a predictable schedule, the comfort of not having to talk to people whom I find difficult or challenging. In men who aspire to eldership, the inclination toward comfort often manifests itself in a desire to control what eldership will require: how much time will it take? What will it demand of me? How can I fit it into my already existing schedule? If you find yourself asking these questions, you may need to examine where comfort has a grip on your soul.

Reflection Question: What comforts do you resist giving up for the sake of ministry?

The seduction of pleasure (escape). Whether it's a hostile church member, a broken marriage, or a downturn in giving, the elders of a church are perpetually immersed in challenging situations. The temptation to escape is strong. When leaders are not resting in the presence, promises, and provision of the Lord Jesus Christ, they will be prone to seek a "quick fix" in sex, food, gambling, entertainment, alcohol, and a host of other momentary pleasures. Men who have had victory over lust for years may find themselves suddenly tempted by pornography. Men who live very disciplined lives may be suddenly tempted by laziness and apathy. Men who haven't ever struggled with drunkenness may find themselves drinking more frequently. Often the temptation toward pleasure goes hand-in-hand with entitlement: "Since I've been working so hard in ministry, I deserve this little indulgence."

Reflection Question: Where do you tend to run when you want to escape?

The seduction of greed. Both 1 Timothy and Titus warn against elders who are "lovers of money." But the character vice of greed doesn't always manifest itself as a lust for financial gain. Among leaders, greed often shows up as *a relentless drive for more*—more people, more money, a growing ministry, a bigger platform, a wider influence. Christians sometimes baptize this sort of greed as a longing for "kingdom growth." But underneath, it's often driven by ego and a thirst for reputation. Paul warns the Ephesian elders that wolves will arise seeking "to draw away the disciples after them" (Acts 20:30). Heart check: Is your desire for growth really about more people meeting Jesus—or is it about you having more followers, more exposure, more influence?

Reflection Question: Where do you see in yourself a relentless drive for more?

The seduction of affirmation. People tend to look up to, respect, and admire their leaders. And this approval and affirmation is inherently seductive. All of us enjoy being liked! If elders are not deeply grounded in God's approval of them, they can begin to find identity in people's approval of them. Their ministry becomes about pleasing people rather than pleasing God. They find themselves adapting to people's preferences and devastated by criticism or conflict.

Reflection Question: Whose affirmation (or lack thereof) has the greatest effect on you?

Perhaps, after reflecting on these five seductions, you're starting to doubt whether you have what it takes. Who wouldn't be seduced by these things? How can you possibly persist in ministry for the long haul without giving in to these temptations?

The grace of the Lord Jesus Christ is the answer. All five of these seductions are rooted in self-glory, self-righteousness, and self-sufficiency. So the way to defeat them is to allow our hearts to rest deeply in the glory, righteousness, and sufficiency of the Lord Jesus.

Jesus is the truly glorious one. He is the one my heart truly longs for—the beauty my soul was made to embrace. The temporary, fleeting satisfactions of pleasure, comfort, affirmation, and ministry growth simply do not and will not fulfill my deepest longings. Their glory pales in comparison to Jesus.

Jesus has given his righteousness to me. My righteousness counts for nothing—all my righteous deeds are like filthy rags (Isaiah 64:6). I come bankrupt to Jesus and am clothed with his righteousness by grace through faith. Therefore, I have no "rights" to demand. I "deserve" nothing. Everything is grace. I'm not entitled to anything, nor do I lack anything, because I am in him (Philippians 3:7–11). I rest in his righteousness when things go well, and I rest in his righteousness when things go poorly.

Jesus is sufficient for all my needs. If I have Jesus, I am rich, though I lack everything else (Philippians 3:8). I need nothing to complete me or make me whole; because of the love of Christ, I am filled with all the fullness of God (Ephesians 3:19). I can be content in seasons of great comfort, affirmation, and ministry success, and I can be content in seasons of suffering and hardship and difficulty—because in every season, I have Christ, and he is sufficient (Philippians 4:11–13).

It's one thing to believe these truths about Jesus. It's another thing to revisit them over and over again until they sink in deeply and begin to affect the fundamental "operating system" of our hearts. A life of gospel ministry is a life of constant communion with Jesus—constantly returning to this good news over and over again. As we believe this good news and let it "get down deep" into our souls, we find that the power of the gospel increasingly frees us to resist the peculiar temptations of leadership.

DISCUSSION QUESTIONS

1. What new insights did this article give you into the contours of these five temptations of leadership (entitlement, comfort, pleasure/escape, greed, affirmation)?

2. When have you seen a leader fall into one of these five seductions? What were the consequences for his life and ministry?

3. Which of the Reflection Questions above resonate most deeply with you? What insights does it give you?

4. Self-glory, self-righteousness, self-sufficiency... Describe what each of these looks like in you—and to others.

5. "It's one thing to believe these truths about Jesus. It's another thing to revisit them over and over again until they sink in deeply." In light of this, how does robust worship—both public and private—help to defeat temptation? Why is passionate worship crucial to healthy leadership?

6. What further questions does this lesson raise for you?

lesson

EXERCISE

IDENTIFYING YOUR TEMPTATIONS

Author and counselor Paul David Tripp, in his book *Dangerous Calling*, observes: "All of us have the tendency in our sin to become very skilled self-swindlers. . . . If you aren't daily admitting to yourself that you are a mess and in daily and rather desperate need for forgiving and transforming grace . . . you are going to give yourself to the work of convincing yourself that you are okay."[1]

The goal of this exercise, then, is to prevent "self-swindling" by helping you grow in self-awareness, specifically in identifying your vulnerability to these five seductions. With that, let's revisit the five reflection questions in the article.

- As a leader, what do you feel entitled to?
- What comforts do you resist giving up for the sake of ministry?
- Where do you tend to run when you want to escape?
- Where do you see in yourself a relentless drive for more?
- Whose affirmation (or lack thereof) has the greatest effect on you?

Based on your answers, which of the five seductions—entitlement, comfort, pleasure, greed, affirmation—have you already experienced? Describe when and how.

What specific shape might each of these seductions take in your *actual* ministry? In other words, What kinds of things would you feel entitled to? What comforts or pleasures would you be prone to seek? If you wanted "more" of something, what would it be? Whose affirmation would you be influenced by? Answer as specifically as you can.

Tripp later goes on to say in *Dangerous Calling*:

> It is only love for Christ that can defend the heart of the pastor against all the other loves that have the potential to kidnap his ministry. It is only worship of Christ that has the power to protect him from all the seductive idols of ministry that will whisper in his ear. It is only the glory of the risen Christ that will guard him against the self-glory that is a temptation to all who are in ministry and destroys the ministry of so many. . . . It is only a heart that is satisfied in Christ that can be spiritually content in the hardships of ministry.[2]

Write a paragraph here about the glories of Christ—specifically, how he's better than the seductions you face. What truths about Jesus most move your heart? What aspects of his person and work are most compelling to you?

CONCLUSION

Congratulations! You've reached the end of this study. And it's my prayer that the Holy Spirit has used it to both encourage and challenge you in your pursuit of eldership. If you've made it to this point, you've taken in a lot of information. Hopefully you have a better, more biblical understanding of eldership. But don't mistake information for transformation.

To further the Spirit's work of transformation, it will be helpful as you conclude this study to spend time in prayer and reflection. Invite the Holy Spirit to confirm some specific, tangible areas where you need further growth and development.

Vision: As you've progressed through this study, what one or two things have you been most challenged or convicted about by the Holy Spirit?

Intention: What are you going do as a result? (Awareness is not the same thing as action!)

Means: What means do you need to apply? What resources or opportunities will you pursue in order to make tangible progress in this area?

Use the next page to write out a prayer expressing your heart before God as you conclude this study. Make sure to date your prayer so you can mark this moment and be encouraged as you revisit it in the future.

APPENDIX A:
FUNCTIONAL & FORMATIVE ELDERSHIP

Eldership is not a destination.

It's important that you know that. Otherwise, you'll treat it as a goal to be reached instead of a stewardship to be exercised. If God is calling you toward eldership, he doesn't just want to work *through* you; he wants to work *in* you. His plan is to sanctify you through eldership.

> Consider it all joy, my brethren, when you encounter various trials, knowing that the testing of your faith produces endurance. And let endurance have its perfect result, so that you may be perfect and complete, lacking in nothing. But if any of you lacks wisdom, let him ask of God, who gives to all generously and without reproach, and it will be given to him. (James 1:2–5 NASB)

Rest assured that eldership will be full of trials. Difficult people, challenging seasons of ministry, church conflict, and satanic opposition will take a toll on the faithful pastor. Leaders are often tempted to see these trials as problems to be solved, obstacles to be overcome, challenges to be met. But God's goal in these trials and tribulations is the formation of your character. He is making you into a certain kind of person. As E. M. Bounds expressed it, "The church is looking for better methods; God is looking for better men."[1] A healthy, gospel-centered view of eldership is not only about ensuring better *ministry*, but about forming better *men*.

In other words, eldership should be both *functional* and *formative*. *Functional* means that it should be effective, productive, and helpful to the mission of the church. *Formative* means that it should contribute to the ongoing spiritual formation of the men who serve as elders.

Why is this ongoing spiritual formation so important? Because the gospel demands it. Colossians 1:6 tells us that the gospel is "continually bearing fruit and growing" in us. All of life is a context for gospel growth. For those of us who lead others, this means that our leadership isn't just about presenting others "mature in Christ" (Colossians 1:28)—it's about growing in our own Christlikeness as well. Elders who see their office as a destination are at high risk of becoming prideful, stagnant, and ineffective. But those who see it as an opportunity for formation are likely to remain humble, teachable, and soft toward the Spirit's work.

Let's consider three dynamics of eldership that are crucial both to the effective *functioning* of an elder team and to the spiritual *formation* of the men who serve on that team.

FIRST AMONG EQUALS

Biblical eldership operates with a first-among-equals dynamic. "Elders act jointly as a council and share equal authority and responsibility . . . [but some] will naturally stand out among the other elders as leaders and teachers within the leadership body."[2] In most cases, the first-among-equals is the lead pastor or main preaching pastor.

One of Satan's primary strategies to hinder the mission of God is to foment tension and division among the elders. Division usually doesn't arise around instances of blatant sin (that's too easily recognized). Rather, it arises through interpersonal differences, disagreements over vision and direction, and smatterings of unresolved conflict that build up over time.

Functionally: How can elders lead in a way that honors both the *first* and the *equal* in a first-among-equals scenario?

Functionally: If you found yourself at odds personally or directionally with the first-among-equals in your church, what would you do?

Formatively: Do you sense hints of pride, selfish ambition, or envy in your heart toward other elders or elder candidates? How will you deal with these feelings in light of the gospel?

RESPONSIBILITY AND ACCOUNTABILITY

Because eldership is the highest office of servant leadership in the church, it comes with a great measure of responsibility. Elders are accountable before God for the souls of the flock and for the progress of God's mission. Elders should be the best leaders in the church, and they should be held accountable for the results of their leadership.

One trend among church leaders that hinders both functionality and formation is the "spiritualization" of the work of ministry. Performance reviews, metrics, and accountability are "unspiritual," it is argued. Since we are doing God's work, we shouldn't try to measure progress. However, if corporations, which exist primarily to make a material profit, hold their leaders and laborers accountable for results, how much more should the church do so in light of the eternal significance of its mission?

Functionally: Why are measures of accountability good for the health and progress of the church? Should metrics be similar to those used in the corporate world or different? Why or why not? If so, in what ways?

Functionally: If an elder is doing poorly in his work, how should the other elders respond?

Formatively: How does having your work measured and evaluated confront idolatry? How should it drive you to "really believe" the gospel?

SEASONS OF LEADERSHIP

One of the greatest hindrances to movement is *stagnation of leadership*. Unless a church is consistently moving men toward eldership, sending men out to plant churches, and leveraging the giftedness of its leaders, it will become a monument instead of a movement.

For a church to maintain a movement spirit, every elder must die to himself. He must care more about the mission than about his own ego. He must have an accurate perception of his gifting. Above all, he must recognize that eldership is an office, not an identity. A man can be *elder-qualified* without serving in the office of elder. Our aspiration before God should be to *qualify* for the office, not necessarily to *hold* the office.

A man who makes a good elder in a church of one hundred may not be such a good elder in a church of one thousand. This does not necessarily mean he is less qualified at the level of character. It simply means that as a church or movement grows, different levels and types of competence and compatibility are required.

Similarly, qualified men may go through seasons of life where they are not able to devote the time and energy necessary to eldership. A man who has a health crisis in his family, or who is raising a special-needs child, or is asked to take on a new level of responsibility at work may not be able to function in the office of elder at the capacity the church needs. Clinging to the office in this sort of scenario reflects a heart of pride and title-lust rather than a humble desire to see the mission go forward.

For eldership to be functional and formative, men must recognize the seasonal nature of leadership. They must be willing to humbly step aside if the needs of the church outpace their giftedness or ability. This is *functional* because it adjusts to the changing nature of ministry. It is *formative* because it builds humility and selflessness that younger leaders can see and emulate. A church full of men who qualify as elders, have served for a season, and have handed the baton to others would be a refreshing anomaly in a culture addicted to pride, power, and position.

> **Functionally**: What do you perceive your "leadership ceiling" to be? In other words, how large of a ministry could you directly oversee—and feel confident of its quality and effectiveness? Do others agree with your perception?

> **Functionally**: What will it look like for you to cultivate a "movement mindset" in your own pursuit of eldership?

> **Formatively**: All of us tend to find a certain sense of identity in titles, offices, and positions that we hold. How does this affect your thinking about eldership? How does the gospel apply to this thinking?

APPENDIX B:
SUPPLEMENTAL RESOURCES

Below is a list of some key resources I've found helpful in the areas of leadership, eldership, and spiritual formation.

THEOLOGICAL AND EXEGETICAL FOUNDATIONS

Strauch, Alexander. *Biblical Eldership*. Colorado Springs: Lewis and Roth Publishers, 1995. This is the industry-standard work on eldership. Strauch exegetes every single passage in the Bible on eldership, unfolding both the theological backbone and the practical realities of shepherding leadership.

Strauch, Alexander. *Biblical Eldership Study Guide*. Littleton, CO: Lewis and Roth Publishers, 1996. This study guide is designed to go along with the book and provide a tool for personal study and reflection.

THEOLOGY IN PRACTICE

Miller, C. John. *Outgrowing the Ingrown Church*. Grand Rapids, MI: Zondervan, 1999. If you've ever used the phrase "gospel-centered," you're living the legacy of Jack Miller. He was writing about the "missional church" before we had language for it. Jack was a church planter, a seminary professor, and a man deeply in touch with his own need for the gospel. He wrote this book to help explain how the gospel brings a church to life.

Ortlund, Ray. *The Gospel: How the Church Portrays the Beauty of Christ.* Wheaton, IL: Crossway, 2014. "Gospel doctrine creates a gospel culture." That's the thrust of this book. Ray wants to help us understand how to shape gospel culture in the churches we lead.

Patrick, Darrin. *Church Planter.* Wheaton, IL: Crossway Books, 2010. For elders working in church-planting contexts, this is a must-read. Darrin has culled and condensed all the best wisdom on "the man, the message, and the mission" of church planting. And he has the stories and scars that prove he knows what he's talking about.

SPIRITUAL AND LEADERSHIP FORMATION

Miller, Paul. *A Praying Life.* Colorado Springs, CO: NavPress, 2009. The most helpful book I've ever read on prayer. Rich, deep, wise, helpful, and saturated with gospel grace.

Powlison, David. "Idols of the Heart & Vanity Fair." *Journal of Biblical Counseling,* vol. 13: 2 (Winter 1995), 35–50. The best and most succinct essay on heart idolatry from a well-respected biblical counselor.

Tripp, Paul David. *Dangerous Calling: Confronting the Unique Challenges of Pastoral Ministry.* Wheaton, IL: Crossway Books, 2012. In his inimitable way, Tripp dives deeply into the particular temptations of pastoral leadership. Every pastor-elder would be well served to read this book and do the heart work it calls for.

Willard, Dallas. *Renovation of the Heart: Putting on the Character of Christ.* Colorado Springs: NavPress, 2002. Hands-down the best book on spiritual formation written during my lifetime. As both an academic philosopher and a Bible-saturated theologian, Willard offers insights into dynamics of formation and re-formation that will change how you think about discipleship.

ENDNOTES

Introduction: What Is an Elder?

1. The best work on this subject is *Recovering Biblical Manhood and Womanhood*, John Piper and Wayne Grudem, eds. (Wheaton, IL: Crossway Books/Council on Biblical Manhood and Womanhood, 2006). Also see Wayne Grudem, *Evangelical Feminism and Biblical Truth* (Wheaton, IL: Crossway, 2012); Mary Cassian, *The Feminist Mistake* (Wheaton, IL: Crossway, 2005); and Peter Kreeft, "Sexual Symbolism," at http://www.peterkreeft.com/topics-more/sexual-symbolism.htm (last accessed 6/22/15).

Lesson 1: Servant Leadership

1. Serge, *Sonship*, 3rd ed. (Greensboro, NC: New Growth Press, 2013), 1–2.

Lesson 2: A Biblical Approach to Church Leadership

1. Dave Harvey, *Am I Called?* (Wheaton, IL: Crossway, 2012), 24–25.

2. Ibid., 52–54.

3. John Piper, "Biblical Eldership, Part 1a: Shepherd the Flock of God Among You," sermon given May 1, 1999, transcribed. http://www.desiringgod.org/messages/biblical-eldership-part-1a#OtherNames.

4. Wayne Grudem, *Systematic Theology* (Grand Rapids, MI: Zondervan, 1994), 911.

5. John Calvin, *Institutes of the Christian Religion*, ed. John T. McNeill, trans. Ford Lewis Battles (Philadelphia: Westminster Press, 1960), 1087 (IV.5.3).

6. Ibid., 1095 (IV.5.11).

7. Alexander Strauch, *Biblical Eldership* (Colorado Springs: Lewis and Roth, 1995), 16.

Lesson 3: The Primacy of Character

1. Dallas Willard, "Idaho Springs Inquiries Concerning Spiritual Formation," http://www.dwillard.org/articles/artview.asp?artID=36 (last accessed 6/24/15).

2. Martin Luther, "The Ninety-Five Theses," http://www.lapham-squarterly.org/revolutions/questioning-pope (last accessed 6/24/15).

3. D. Martyn Lloyd-Jones, "Idolatry," in *Life in God: Studies in 1 John* (Wheaton, IL: Crossway, 2002), 728–29.

4. The chart that follows is adapted from Darrin Patrick, *Church Planter* (Wheaton, IL: Crossway, 2010), 162–67. In a footnote, Patrick acknowledges that he's building upon the work of Dick Kaufman (in unpublished lectures) and Dick Keyes (in the book *No God But God*, ed. Os Guinness and John Seel [Chicago: Moody Press, 1992]).

Lesson 4: The Leadership Triangle

1. John M. Frame, *The Doctrine of the Knowledge of God* (Phillipsburg, NJ: P&R Publishing, 1987). Thanks also to David Fairchild, pastor of Trinity Church West Seattle, for his insights into applying Frame's grid to eldership.

2. From David Fairchild's white paper, "Triperspectival Leadership Essentials," obtained through personal correspondence with the author.

Interlude: The Duties of Elders

1. Strauch, *Biblical Eldership*, 15–34.

Lesson 5: Elders Feed the Church

1. Alan D. Lieberson, "How Long Can a Person Survive without Food," *Scientific American*, November 8, 2004, http://www.scientificamerican.com/article.cfm?id=how-long-can-a-person-sur (last accessed 6/24/15).

2. David Powlison, *Seeing with New Eyes* (Phillipsburg, NJ: P&R Publishing, 2003), 29.

3. Paul Miller, *A Praying Life* (Colorado Springs: NavPress, 2009), 57.

4. Haddon Robinson, *Biblical Preaching* (Grand Rapids, MI: Baker Book House, 1980), 24.

5. Powlison, *Seeing with New Eyes*, 40–43.

6. Ibid., 24.

Lesson 6: Elders Lead the Church

1. Derek Tidball, *Skillful Shepherds: Explorations in Pastoral Theology* (Leicester, UK: APOLLOS/Inter-Varsity, 1997), 337.

2. J. Oswald Sanders, *Spiritual Leadership*, rev. ed. (Chicago: Moody Press, 1989), 25–26.

3. Ibid., 35.

4. Leonard Sax, *Boys Adrift* (New York: Basic Books, 2007), 163, 167.

Lesson 7: Elders Protect the Church

1. Quoted in Strauch, *Biblical Eldership*, 145.

2. Richard Lovelace, *Dynamics of Spiritual Life* (Downers Grove, IL: InterVarsity Press, 1979), 219.

3. John Owen, *Mortification of Sin*, 6.2.2, http://www.ccel.org/ccel/owen/mort.i.ix.html (last accessed 7/1/15).

4. Quoted in Strauch, *Biblical Eldership*, 145.

5. Owen, *Mortification of Sin*, 2.1.1.

6. D. Martyn Lloyd-Jones, *Studies in the Sermon on the Mount*, 2nd ed. (Grand Rapids, MI: Eerdmans, 1976), 500.

7. Lovelace, *Dynamics of Spiritual Life*, 74.

Lesson 8: Elders Care for the Church

1. Derek Tidball, *Skillful Shepherds*, 100.

2. Ibid., 99–100.

3. Eugene H. Peterson, *The Contemplative Pastor: Returning to the Art of Spiritual Direction* (Grand Rapids, MI: Eerdmans, 1993), 17.

4. Ibid., 21.

5. Alexander Strauch, *Biblical Eldership Study Guide* (Littleton, CO: Lewis and Roth, 1996), 174.

Lesson 9: Missional Eldership

1. Peter Kreeft, *Christianity for Modern Pagans* (San Francisco: Ignatius Press, 1993), 12–13.

Lesson 10: The Temptations of Leadership

1. Paul David Tripp, *Dangerous Calling* (Wheaton, IL: Crossway, 2012), 33.

2. Ibid., 64.

Appendix A: Functional & Formative Eldership

1. E. M. Bounds, *Power through Prayer* (Grand Rapids, MI: Baker Book House, 2001), 11.

2. Strauch, *Biblical Eldership*, 45.